Teacher's Editic

# Reading Routines COMPANION

## Practices Grounded in the Science of Reading

**Developed in collaboration with Dr. Sharon Vaughn**

In consultation with
Dr. Elfrieda H. Hiebert, Dr. P. David Pearson,
Dr. Frank Serafini, and Dr. Judy Wallis

3

myView®
LITERACY

SAVVAS
LEARNING COMPANY

Savvas Learning Company LLC, 15 East Midland Avenue, Paramus, NJ 07652



SAVVAS
LEARNING COMPANY

ISBN-13: 978-1-4285-5371-2
ISBN-10: 1-4285-5371-1

Printed in Mexico 1 23

# Table of Contents, Grade 3

# *myView Literacy* Crosswalk

| Word Study Routines | *myView* Crosswalk |
|---|---|
| Syllable Pattern VC/CV, pp. 57–58 | **Unit 1, Week 1,** pp. T22, T54, T62, T70, T76; **Week 2,** p. T132 |
| Inflected Endings *-s, -es, -ies,* pp. 59–60 | **Unit 1, Week 2,** pp. T92, T116, T124; **Week 3,** p. T194 |
| Base Words and Endings *-ing, -ed, -er, -est,* pp. 61–62 | **Unit 1, Week 3,** pp. T154, T178, T186, T200; **Week 4,** p. T264 |
| Vowel Digraphs *ee, ea, ai, ay, ow, oa,* pp. 63–64 | **Unit 1, Week 4,** pp. T216, T248, T256, T270; **Week 5,** p. T326 |
| Diphthongs *ou, ow, oi, oy,* pp. 65–66 | **Unit 1, Week 5,** pp. T286, T310, T318, T332; **Unit 2, Week 1,** p. T62 |
| Syllable Patterns VC/V and V/CV, pp. 67–68 | **Unit 2, Week 1,** pp. T22, T46, T54, T68; **Week 2,** p. T124 |
| *r*-Controlled Vowels *ar, or, ore, oar,* pp. 69–70 | **Unit 2, Week 2,** pp. T84, T108, T116, T130; **Week 3,** p. T184 |
| Compound Words, pp. 71–72 | **Unit 2, Week 3,** pp. T146, T168, T176, T190; **Week 4,** p. T246 |
| Syllable Pattern VCe, pp. 73–74 | **Unit 2, Week 4,** pp. T206, T230, T238, T252; **Week 5,** p. T308 |
| Contractions, pp. 75–76 | **Unit 2, Week 5,** pp. T268, T292, T300, T314; **Unit 3, Week 1,** p. T70 |
| Prefixes *pre-, dis-, in-, im-, non-,* pp. 77–78 | **Unit 3, Week 1,** pp. T22, T54, T62, T76; **Week 2,** p. T130 |
| Abbreviations, pp. 79–80 | **Unit 3, Week 2,** pp. T92, T114, T122, T136; **Week 3,** p. T192 |
| Suffixes *-ful, -y, -ness,* pp. 81–82 | **Unit 3, Week 3,** pp. T152, T176, T184, T198; **Week 4,** p. T252 |
| Vowel Teams *oo, ew, ue, ui, eu,* pp. 83–84 | **Unit 3, Week 4,** pp. T214, T236, T244, T258; **Week 5,** p. T310 |
| Irregular Plurals, pp. 85–86 | **Unit 3, Week 5,** pp. T274, T294, T302, T316; **Unit 4, Week 1,** p. T64 |

| Word Study Routines | *myView* Crosswalk |
|---|---|
| *r*-Controlled Vowels *ir, er, ur, ear,* pp. 87–88 | **Unit 4, Week 1,** pp. T22, T48, T56, T70; **Week 2,** p. T124 |
| VCCCV Pattern, pp. 89–90 | **Unit 4, Week 2,** pp. T86, T108, T116, T130; **Week 3,** p. T188 |
| Latin Suffixes *-able, -ible, -ation,* pp. 91–92 | **Unit 4, Week 3,** pp. T146, T172, T180, T194; **Week 4,** p. T254 |
| Homographs, pp. 93–94 | **Unit 4, Week 4,** pp. T210, T238, T246, T260; **Week 5,** p. T316 |
| Homophones, pp. 95–96 | **Unit 4, Week 5,** pp. T276, T300, T308, T322; **Unit 5, Week 1,** p. T66 |
| Vowel Patterns *au, aw, al, augh, ough,* pp. 97–98 | **Unit 5, Week 1,** pp. T22, T50, T58, T72; **Week 2,** p. T124 |
| Vowel Patterns *ei, eigh,* pp. 99–100 | **Unit 5, Week 2,** pp. T88, T108, T116, T130; **Week 3,** p. T184 |
| Words with Suffix *-en,* pp. 101–102 | **Unit 5, Week 3,** pp. T146, T168, T176, T190; **Week 4,** p. T252 |
| Schwa, pp. 103–104 | **Unit 5, Week 4,** pp. T206, T236, T244, T252; **Week 5,** p. T314 |
| Final Stable Syllables *-le, -ture, -ive, -ize,* pp. 105–106 | **Unit 5, Week 5,** pp. T274, T298, T306, T320 |

| Vocabulary Routines | *myView* Crosswalk |
|---|---|
| Oral Vocabulary: Build Background Knowledge, pp. 135–136 | Use with Listening Comprehension lessons |
| Use Resources, pp. 137–138 | **Unit 1, Week 2,** p. T90; p. T474; **Unit 2, Week 2,** p. T82; **Unit 3, Week 2,** p. T90; **Unit 4, Week 2,** p. T84 |
| Context Clues: Synonyms, pp. 139–140 | **Unit 1, Week 2,** p. T90; **Week 3,** p. T152; **Unit 2, Week 2,** p. T82; **Week 3,** p. T144; **Unit 3, Week 2,** p. T90; **Week 3,** p. T150; **Unit 4, Week 2,** p. T84; **Week 3,** p. T144; **Unit 5, Week 2,** p. T86; **Week 3,** p. T144 |
| Context Clues: Antonyms, pp. 141–142 | **Unit 1, Week 2,** p. T90; **Week 3,** p. T152; **Unit 2, Week 2,** p. T82; **Week 3,** p. T144; **Unit 3, Week 2,** p. T90; **Week 3,** p. T150; **Unit 4, Week 2,** p. T84; **Week 3,** p. T144; **Unit 5, Week 2,** p. T86; **Week 3,** p. T144 |
| Context Clues: Surrounding Text, pp. 143–144 | **Unit 1, Week 3,** p. T152; **Unit 2, Week 3,** p. T144; **Unit 3, Week 3,** p. T150; **Unit 4, Week 3,** p. T144; **Unit 5, Week 3,** p. T144 |
| Word Parts for Meaning, pp. 145–146 | **Unit 1, Week 1,** p. T20; **Unit 2, Week 1,** p. T20; **Week 3,** pp. T146, T168, T176, T190; **Week 4,** p. T246; **Unit 3, Week 1,** pp. T20, T22, T54, T62, T76; **Week 2,** p. T130; **Week 3,** pp. T152, T176, T184, T198; **Week 4,** p. T252; **Unit 4, Week 1,** p. T20; **Week 3,** pp. T146, T172, T180, T194; **Week 4,** p. T254; **Unit 5, Week 1,** p. T20; **Week 3,** pp. T146, T168, T176, T190; **Week 4,** p. T252 |
| Figurative Language: Similes, pp. 147–148 | **Unit 1, Week 1,** p. T60; **Week 4,** p. T214; **Unit 2, Week 4,** p. T204; **Unit 3, Week 4,** p. T212; **Unit 5, Week 4,** p. T204 |
| Figurative Language: Metaphors, pp. 149–150 | **Unit 1, Week 4,** p. T236; **Unit 2, Week 4,** p. T223; **Unit 3, Week 4,** p. T232 |
| Figurative Language: Analogies, pp. 151–152 | **Unit 4, Week 4,** p. T208 |

| Fluency Routines | *myView* Crosswalk |
|---|---|
| **Accuracy,** pp. 155–156 | Use with Small Group, Lessons 2–4 |
| **Rate,** pp. 157–158 | Use with Small Group, Lessons 2–4 |
| **Prosody: Poetry,** pp. 159–160 | **Unit 3, Week 5,** pp. T304, T312 |
| **Prosody: Narrative Texts,** pp. 161–162 | **Unit 1, Week 1,** pp. T56, T64, T72; **Week 2,** p. T134; **Week 3,** pp. T180, T188, T196; **Week 5,** pp. T312, T320, T328; **Unit 2, Week 3,** pp. T170, T178, T186; **Unit 3, Week 1,** pp. T56, T64, T72; **Week 2,** pp. T116, T124, T132; **Week 3,** pp. T178, T186, T194; **Week 4,** pp. T238, T246, T254; **Unit 4, Week 1,** pp. T50, T58, T66; **Week 2,** pp. T110, T118, T126; **Week 3,** pp. T174, T182; **Week 4,** pp. T240, T248, T256; **Unit 5, Week 4,** pp. T238, T246, T254; **Week 5,** pp. T300, T308, T316 |
| **Prosody: Informational Texts,** pp. 163–164 | **Unit 1, Week 4,** pp. T250, T258, T266; **Unit 2, Week 1,** pp. T48, T56, T64; **Week 2,** pp. T110, T118, T126; **Week 4,** pp. T232, T240, T248; **Week 5,** pp. T294, T302, T310; **Unit 3, Week 4,** pp. T238, T246, T254; **Unit 4, Week 1,** pp. T50, T58, T66; **Week 2,** pp. T110, T118, T126; **Week 3,** pp. T174, T182; **Week 4,** pp. T240, T248, T256; **Unit 5, Week 1,** pp. T52, T60, T68; **Week 2,** pp. T110, T118, T126; **Week 3,** pp. T170, T178, T186 |
| **Prosody: Drama,** pp. 165–166 | **Unit 4, Week 5,** pp. T302, T310, T318 |
| **Fluency and Qualitative Measures,** pp. 167–168 | Use with *Cold Reads for Fluency and Comprehension* |
| **Target Fluency Goals,** p. 169 | Use with *Cold Reads for Fluency and Comprehension* |
| **Oral Reading Fluency Rubric,** p. 170 | Use with *Cold Reads for Fluency and Comprehension* |

| Comprehension Routines | *myView* Crosswalk |
|---|---|
| Build Background Knowledge, pp. 179–180 | Use with Introduce the Text lessons; *see also* **Unit 3, Week 2,** p. T126; **Unit 4, Week 4,** p. T250; **Unit 5, Week 4,** p. T248 |
| Ask and Answer Questions, pp. 181–182 | **Unit 1, Week 2,** p. T128; **Unit 4, Week 3,** p. T184 |
| Predictions, pp. 183–184 | **Unit 3, Week 1,** p. T66; **Unit 4, Week 1,** p. T60; **Unit 5, Week 1,** p. T62 |
| Make Inferences, pp. 185–186 | **Unit 1, Week 2,** p. T120; **Week 3,** p. T190; **Unit 3, Week 3,** p. T180; **Unit 4, Week 2,** p. T120; **Unit 5, Week 5,** p. T302 |
| Main Idea and Details, pp. 187–188 | **Unit 2, Week 1,** p. T50; **Unit 4, Week 2,** p. T112 |
| Monitor Comprehension, pp. 189–190 | **Unit 2, Week 1,** p. T58; **Unit 3, Week 5,** p. T306; **Unit 4, Week 5,** p. T312; **Unit 5, Week 3,** p. T180 |
| Summarize, pp. 191–192 | **Unit 3, Week 4,** p. T248 |
| Synthesize, pp. 193–194 | **Unit 2, Week 3,** p. T180; **Unit 5, Week 2,** p. T120 |
| Text Structure: Chronological/Sequence, pp. 195–196 | **Unit 3, Week 4,** p. T220; **Unit 4, Week 1,** p. T52; **Week 4,** p. T244 |
| Text Structure: Description, pp. 197–198 | **Unit 5, Week 2,** p. T85 |
| Text Structure: Steps in a Process, pp. 199–200 | **Unit 5, Week 3,** p. T174 |
| Text Structure: Cause and Effect, pp. 201–202 | **Unit 2, Week 5,** p. T298; **Unit 5, Week 2,** p. T112; **Week 3,** pp. T172 |

# Instruction Grounded in Research

You are likely wondering, as are many educators, *what is the science of reading and how do I know if the program I'm using is responsive to the science of reading?* The science of reading is based on a cumulative and evolving set of evidence that is derived from studies built upon the scientific method. This evidence is useful in making decisions about what to teach and also in many cases, how to teach.

Some of the knowledge about learning to read is indisputable and would be expected to be a critical part of every reading program. There are several critical features to consider:

- ☑ The science of reading has established that there are critical elements of reading instruction that contribute to the successful acquisition of reading. Sometimes, these elements are referred to as "the big five" – phonological/phonemic awareness, phonics, fluency, vocabulary, and comprehension. However, these are not the only elements that contribute to reading success. Evidence also supports the reciprocal connection between learning to read and learning to spell and write.
- ☑ The emphasis on the critical elements of reading instruction may vary based on the differential needs of the reader – however, the vast majority of learners benefit from the organized, deliberate, and explicit instruction in the critical elements of reading.
- ☑ The science of reading has established that the explicitness of instruction is associated with beneficial outcomes for students. This explicitness includes modeling new skills, giving students ample practice with feedback, and providing structured opportunities for review and practice.
- ☑ The ultimate goal of reading, reading comprehension, is a product of both word decoding and linguistic comprehension – both are required for youngsters to acquire meaning from text.
- ☑ Teaching youngsters phonological awareness combined with letter knowledge improves word-decoding skills. Teaching students explicitly to apply phonics rules improves their word-decoding skills. Students also need to know or acquire the meaning of these words and to understand them in texts (i.e., linguistic comprehension).

**Sharon Vaughn, Ph.D.**
The University of Texas at Austin
myView Literacy Author

# Meet Your *Reading Routines* Companion

This unparalleled companion to your myView Literacy Teacher's Edition provides additional explicit instruction to deepen your whole group and small group lessons. A systematic four-step routine introduces the skill, allows for teacher modeling, and supports guided and extended practice.

**myView Literacy Lesson Connection**

**Explicit Teacher Talk**

SIDE A

PHONOLOGICAL AND PHONEMIC AWARENESS
GRADE 1

## Isolate Phonemes: Medial /a/

**Phoneme isolation** is the ability to identify individual sounds (phonemes) at the beginning, middle, and end of words.

**Connect to *myView Literacy*:**
**Medial /a/:** Unit 1, p. T14

### ROUTINE

**STEP 1 INTRODUCE**

Gather three counters. Today we will listen for the sound /a/ in the middle of words. The middle sound is the sound between the first and last sounds.

**STEP 2 MODEL**

- I will say a word. Listen carefully to the middle sound: *pan*. Have students repeat the word.
- Segment the sounds of the word, placing a counter from left to right as you say each phoneme: /p/ /a/ /n/. Sweep your hand under the counters as you say: *pan*.
- Point to each counter as you say: /p/ /a/ /n/, *pan*. The middle sound in *pan* is /a/. Say the middle sound in *pan* with me: /a/.

**STEP 3 GUIDE PRACTICE**

Provide students with counters to segment the sounds of the word *cap* with you. Point to each counter and have students say the sounds with you: /k/ /a/ /p/. Sweep your hand under the counters: *cap*. What is the middle sound in *cap*? (/a/)

**STEP 4 ON THEIR OWN**

Have students segment the sounds in these words and identify the middle sound.

| | | | | | |
|---|---|---|---|---|---|
| bat | jam | tab | rag | ham | fan |



Isolate P

SIDE B

FLUENCY
GRADE 1

## Rate

**CORRECTIVE FEEDBACK**

| | |
|---|---|
| **IF** students cannot read aloud at an appropriate rate, | **THEN** model how to read aloud at an appropriate rate, using Steps 2 and 3. Next, work through the Make It Easier activity. |

### Make It Easier

Students who cannot read aloud at an appropriate rate may benefit from a word-recognition activity.

- Make a set of word cards of the decodable words from the text and another set of the high-frequency words from the text.
- Start with the decodable words and guide students in blending the sounds for each word. Then use the cards as flashcards and have students read aloud the words until they read them at an appropriate rate.
- Repeat using the high-frequency words.
- Have students read aloud the short text again until they make their reading "sound like talking."

### Make It Harder

Students who can read aloud at an appropriate rate may enjoy reading aloud with a partner.

- Have each partner choose a short text in an appropriate leveled reader.
- Have partners take turns reading aloud their texts so their reading sounds like they are talking. Tell the other partner to listen carefully so he or she can ask the reader a question about the text.
- After each partner has read aloud and answered a question, have partners exchange texts and repeat the activity.



Includes routines for Phonological and Phonemic Awareness, Phonics, Word Study, Fluency, Vocabulary, Comprehension, Dictation, High-Frequency Words, Syllable Patterns, and more!

**Grade 1 Example**

**“The science of reading has established that the explicitness of instruction is associated with beneficial outcomes for students. This explicitness includes modeling new skills, giving students ample practice with feedback, and providing structured opportunities for review and practice.”**

—Dr. Sharon Vaughn

Connected Digital Practice

Targeted feedback that is guided and corrective

Differentiation to meet the range of learners in your classroom

Grade 3 Example

SIDE A

SYLLABLE PATT

## Closed and Open Syllables: Reading

Applying syllabication skills to reading leads to increased fluency and stronger comprehension.

### ROUTINE

See digital practice on SavvasRealize.com.

**STEP 1 INTRODUCE**

Today we are going to use what we have learned about closed and open syllables to help us while we read.

**STEP 2 MODEL**

- I am going to read this sentence. If I come to words I don’t know, I will look for closed and open syllables to help me read the words. Read the sentence. Pause at *lizards.* I am not sure what this word is. I see the vowel *i* and the consonant *z* after the vowel. Sound out /liz/ with emphasis on the sound /i/ and the consonant *z.* /liz/ is a closed syllable, so the first syllable in this word is /liz/. This word is *lizards.* Continue reading.
- Pause at *giant.* I am not sure what this word is. I see the vowel *i,* but there is no consonant after it. I wonder if this word has an open syllable. Sound out /gi/ with emphasis on the sound /ī/. /gi/ is an open syllable, so the first syllable in this word is /gi/. This word is *giant.* Finish reading the sentence and then reread.

**STEP 3 GUIDE PRACTICE**

Let’s read this sentence together. If we come to words we don’t know, we will pause and use our knowledge of closed and open syllables to help us read the words. Use the instruction in Step 2 to guide the students’ reading of the sentence at the right. Pause at *victory* (closed syllable, /vic/) and *remote* (open syllable, /re/).

**STEP 4 ON THEIR OWN**

Ask students to read the sentences at the right. Remind them to look for closed and open syllables to help them.





SIDE B

SYLLABLE PATTERNS
GRADE 3

## Closed and Open Syllables: Reading

**CORRECTIVE FEEDBACK**

| | |
|---|---|
| **IF** students cannot read closed and open syllables in sentences, | **THEN** model how to read closed and open syllables, using Steps 2 and 3. Next, work through the Make It Easier activity on Side B. |

### Make It Easier

Students who cannot read words with closed and open syllables may benefit from more explicit instruction on identifying open syllables.

- Display the word *predict.* Let’s read this word together: *predict. Predict* begins with an open syllable, /pre/. It is an open syllable because it ends with a long vowel sound, /ē/. Underline the vowel *e.* Let’s say the open syllable together: /pre/. Now, let’s read the whole word together: *predict.*
- Display the word *notice.* Let’s read this word together: *notice.* What is the first syllable in *notice?* (/no/) Is /no/ a closed or an open syllable? (open) How do you know? (It is an open syllable because it ends with a long vowel sound, /ō/.) Underline the vowel *o.* Let’s say the open syllable together: /no/. Now, let’s read the whole word together: *notice.*
- Repeat with the words at the right. Call on individual students to read the words. Then, ask students to identify the open syllable in each word. Ask them to underline the open syllable.

predict

notice

behind

decide

pho/to

### Make It Harder

Students who can read closed and open syllables can extend the activity by writing and reading extended sentences.

- Ask students to work with a partner. Each student should write a sentence with at least two multisyllabic words. One word should have a closed syllable. Another word should have an open syllable.
- Partners should exchange sentences and then take turns reading the sentences. Students should identify closed and open syllables in

# Connected Resources for Whole and Small Group Instruction

Solid routines are a key ingredient in every classroom! Strengthen routines and deepen instruction with your *myView Literacy* Teacher's Edition and *Reading Routines Companion.*

## Instruction is Connected!

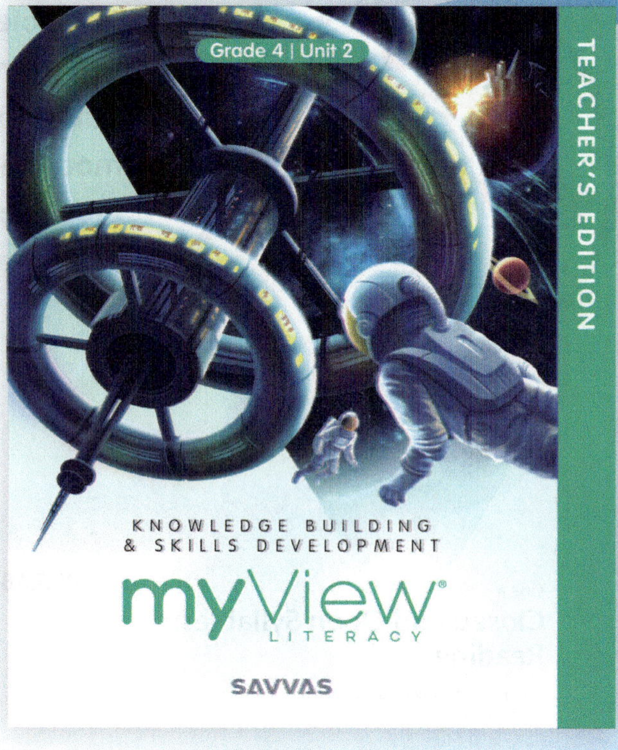


## Teacher's Edition

Core lessons launch instruction and help you deliver an explicit skill with an easy, consistent routine:

1. Teach *(I Do!)*
2. Model and Guide Practice *(We Do!)*
3. Practice *(You Do!)*

**Explicit Teacher Talk**

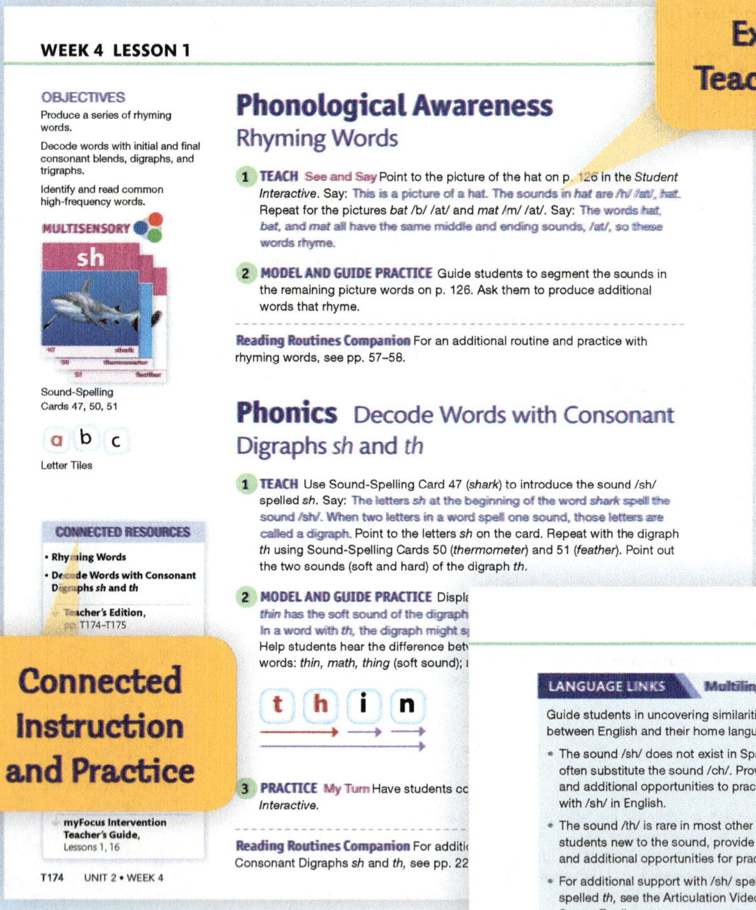

WEEK 4 LESSON 1

OBJECTIVES

Produce a series of rhyming words.

Decode words with initial and final consonant blends, digraphs, and trigraphs.

Identify and read common high-frequency words.

MULTISENSORY

Sound-Spelling Cards 47, 50, 51

Letter Tiles

CONNECTED RESOURCES

- Rhyming Words
- Decode Words with Consonant Digraphs *sh* and *th*

Teacher's Edition, pp. T174–T175

myFocus Intervention Teacher's Guide, Lessons 1, 16

### Phonological Awareness
Rhyming Words

1 **TEACH** See and Say Point to the picture of the hat on p. 126 in the *Student Interactive*. Say: This is a picture of a hat. The sounds in *hat* are /h/ /at/, *hat*. Repeat for the pictures *bat* /b/ /at/ and *mat* /m/ /at/. Say: The words *hat, bat,* and *mat* all have the same middle and ending sounds, /at/, so these words rhyme.

2 **MODEL AND GUIDE PRACTICE** Guide students to segment the sounds in the remaining picture words on p. 126. Ask them to produce additional words that rhyme.

**Reading Routines Companion** For an additional routine and practice with rhyming words, see pp. 57–58.

### Phonics Decode Words with Consonant Digraphs *sh* and *th*

1 **TEACH** Use Sound-Spelling Card 47 (*shark*) to introduce the sound /sh/ spelled *sh*. Say: The letters *sh* at the beginning of the word *shark* spell the sound /sh/. When two letters in a word spell one sound, those letters are called a digraph. Point to the letters *sh* on the card. Repeat with the digraph *th* using Sound-Spelling Cards 50 (*thermometer*) and 51 (*feather*). Point out the two sounds (soft and hard) of the digraph *th*.

2 **MODEL AND GUIDE PRACTICE** Displ
*thin* has the soft sound of the digraph
In a word with *th*, the digraph might s
Help students hear the difference bet
words: *thin, math, thing* (soft sound);

t h i n

3 **PRACTICE** My Turn Have students c
*Interactive.*

**Reading Routines Companion** For additi
Consonant Digraphs *sh* and *th*, see pp. 22

T174 UNIT 2 • WEEK 4

**Connected Instruction and Practice**

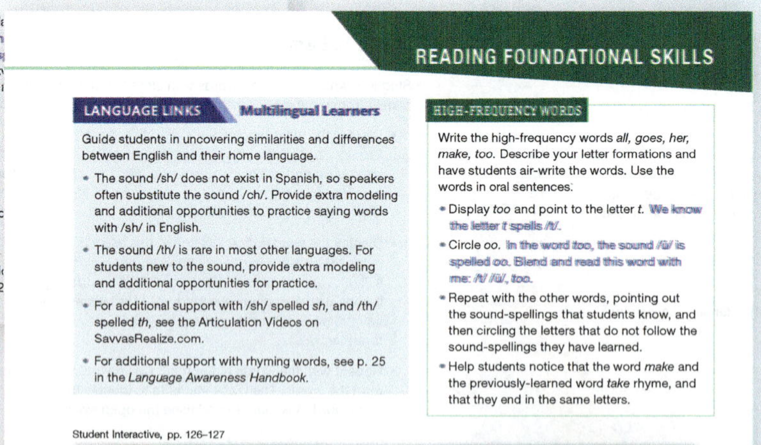

READING FOUNDATIONAL SKILLS

LANGUAGE LINKS Multilingual Learners

Guide students in uncovering similarities and differences between English and their home language.

- The sound /sh/ does not exist in Spanish, so speakers often substitute the sound /ch/. Provide extra modeling and additional opportunities to practice saying words with /sh/ in English.
- The sound /th/ is rare in most other languages. For students new to the sound, provide extra modeling and additional opportunities for practice.
- For additional support with /sh/ spelled *sh*, and /th/ spelled *th*, see the Articulation Videos on SavvasRealize.com.
- For additional support with rhyming words, see p. 25 in the *Language Awareness Handbook*.

HIGH-FREQUENCY WORDS

Write the high-frequency words *all, goes, her, make, too*. Describe your letter formations and have students air-write the words. Use the words in oral sentences.

- Display *too* and point to the letter *t*. We know the letter *t* spells /t/.
- Circle *oo*. In the word *too*, the sound /ü/ is spelled *oo*. Blend and read this word with me: /t/ /ü/, *too*.
- Repeat with the other words, pointing out the sound-spellings that students know, and then circling the letters that do not follow the sound-spellings they have learned.
- Help students notice that the word *make* and the previously-learned word *take* rhyme, and that they end in the same letters.

Student Interactive, pp. 126–127

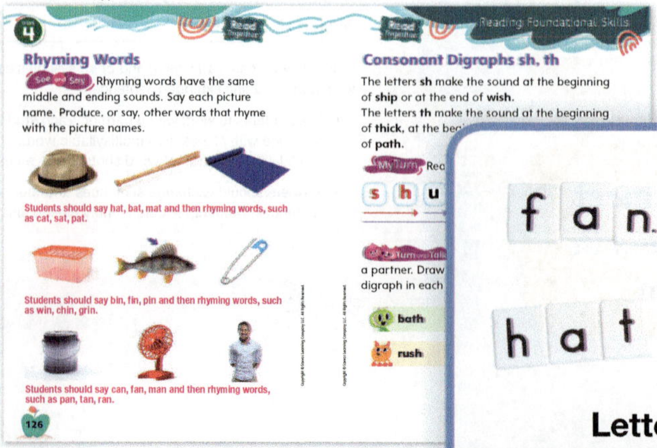

Reading Foundational Skills

**Rhyming Words**

See and Say Rhyming words have the same middle and ending sounds. Say each picture name. Produce, or say, other words that rhyme with the picture names.

Students should say hat, bat, mat and then rhyming words, such as cat, sat, pat.

Students should say bin, fin, pin and then rhyming words, such as win, chin, grin.

Students should say can, fan, man and then rhyming words, such as pan, tan, ran.

126

**Consonant Digraphs sh, th**

The letters **sh** make the sound at the beginning of **ship** or at the end of **wish**.
The letters **th** make the sound at the beginning of **thick**, at the beg
of **path**.

My Turn Rea

s h u

Turn and Talk
a partner. Draw
digraph in each

bath

rush

## Student Practice

The Student Edition includes full color practice pages for each minilesson.

Letter Tiles

**Pair with resources from your Foundational Skills Kit.**

**Multisensory Activities Grades K-2**

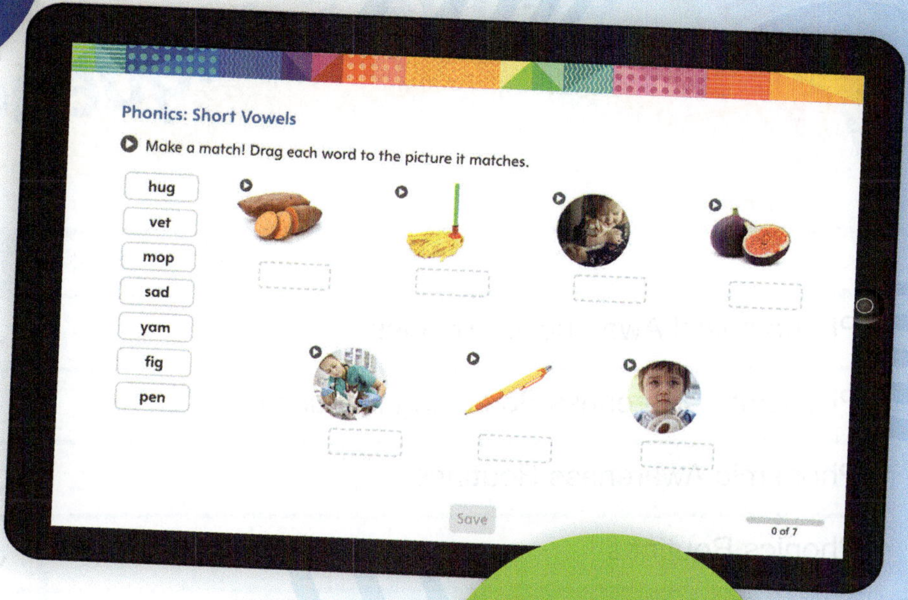


**Digital Practice Activities to Reinforce Skills Grades K-5**

**Routines directly connected to core lessons!**

SIDE A

## Initial Consonant Digraphs *sh, th*

**PHONICS**
GRADE 1

A **consonant digraph** is a single sound represented by two consonants.

**Connect to *myView Literacy*: Decode and Write Wo Consonant Digraphs s**
Unit 2, p. T174

**See digital practice on Savvas**

## ROUTINE

**STEP 1 INTRODUCE**

A consonant digraph is two consonants that spell one sound. Display the digraphs *sh* and *th*. Point to *sh* as you say: The consonants *s* and *h* together spell the sound /sh/. Point to digraph *th* as you say: The consonants *t* and *h* together spell the soft sound /th/ in *thin* or the hard sound /th/ in *they*. Have students say each sound. Today we will read words that begin with the consonant digraphs *sh* and *th*.

sh

th

**STEP 2 MODEL**

- Display the word *shin*. This is how I read the word *shin*. Point to the sound spelling *sh*: Remember, *s* and *h* together spell the one sound /sh/. Say it with me: /sh/. Point to each sound spelling as you say its sound: /sh/ /i/ /n/. Then sweep your hand under *shin* as you blend the sounds and read the word: /sh/ /i/ /n/, *shin*. Model how to write *shin*.
- Repeat for digraph *th*, using the word *thin*.

sh i n

**STEP 3 GUIDE PRACTICE**

- Display the word *thud*: Let's try this word. Point to each sound spelling and have students say the sound with you. Then sweep your hand under *thud* as students decode the word with you: /th/ /u/ /d/, *thud*. Ask: What sound do *t* and *h* together spell at the beginning of *thud*? (/th/) Have students write *thud* with you.
- Repeat for these words: *ship, thick, shot, this, shed,* and *then*.

th u d

**STEP 4 ON THEIR OWN**

Have students decode and write these words: *shop, them, shut, thick, shelf, this*.



Initial Consonant Digr

SIDE B

## Initial Consonant Digraphs *sh, th*

**PHONICS**
GRADE 1

**CORRECTIVE FEEDBACK**

**IF** students cannot decode words with initial digraph *sh* or *th*,

**THEN** model how to decode words with initial digraph *sh* or *th*, using Steps 2 and 3. Next, work through the Make It Easier activity.

### Make It Easier

Some students may need practice with the sound spellings.

- Display letter tiles or cards for the word *this*, leaving space between each letter. Point to *t* and *h*. Then push the two letters together as you say: The letters *t* and *h* work together to spell /th/. Say it with me: /th/, /th/, /th/. Point to *i* and *s* as you say: /i/ /s/. Push the *th* letter tiles into the *i* and *s* tiles as you blend the sounds in the word: /th/ /i/ /s/, *this*. Have students say the word with you.
- Provide each student with a set of letter tiles or cards. Using the words below, have students segment each digraph and letter sound and then push the tiles together as they say the word.

t h i s

th i s

thud ship them shop thin shelf

### Make It Harder

Students who can decode words with initial digraphs *sh* and *th* may be ready to build other words that contain initial *sh* and *th*.

- Provide partners with a set of letter tiles or cards.
- Have partners take turns building a word with initial digraph *sh* or initial digraph *th*. Students may build words such as *shin, ship, shop, shack, shed, shut, shot, shelf, shift, thin, that, thick, then, this, them,* and *thud*.
- Have partners challenge each other in reading aloud each word they build.

# Scope & Sequence

| | K | 1 | 2 | 3 | 4 | 5 |
|---|---|---|---|---|---|---|
| Phonological Awareness Routines | ✓ | ✓ | ✓ | | | |
| Phonemic Awareness Screening Routines | | | | ✓ | ✓ | ✓ |
| Phonemic Awareness Routines | ✓ | ✓ | ✓ | ✓ | ✓ | ✓ |
| Phonics Routines | ✓ | ✓ | ✓ | | | |
| Word Study Routines | | | | ✓ | ✓ | ✓ |
| Dictation Routines | ✓ | ✓ | | | | |
| Vocabulary Routines | ✓ | ✓ | ✓ | ✓ | ✓ | ✓ |
| High-Frequency Word Decoding Routines | ✓ | ✓ | ✓ | ✓ | ✓ | ✓ |
| Syllable Pattern Routines | ✓ | ✓ | ✓ | ✓ | ✓ | ✓ |
| Fluency Routines | ✓ | ✓ | ✓ | ✓ | ✓ | ✓ |
| Self-Monitoring Routine: Oral Reading | | ✓ | ✓ | ✓ | ✓ | ✓ |
| Self-Monitoring Routine: Silent Reading | | | ✓ | ✓ | ✓ | ✓ |
| Comprehension Routines | ✓ | ✓ | ✓ | ✓ | ✓ | ✓ |
| Digital Practice Activities | ✓ | ✓ | ✓ | ✓ | ✓ | ✓ |
| Alphabet Tiles | ✓ | ✓ | ✓ | | | |
| Multisensory Activities | ✓ | ✓ | ✓ | | | |
| Phonics Generalizations | ✓ | ✓ | ✓ | | | |
| Articulation Support Guide | ✓ | ✓ | ✓ | ✓ | ✓ | ✓ |
| Glossary | ✓ | ✓ | ✓ | ✓ | ✓ | ✓ |
| Research | ✓ | ✓ | ✓ | ✓ | ✓ | ✓ |

# Phonemic Awareness

## Guidelines for Phonemic Awareness Routines

Research suggests that most students acquire phonemic awareness, a part of phonological awareness, by the end of first grade. Proficient, automatic phonemic awareness allows students to focus their cognitive energies on decoding and understanding what they read.

Students whose phonemic awareness skills are not yet proficient may benefit from additional direct instruction and practice to internalize the skills. The following Routines allow you to address individual student needs.

Keep these guidelines in mind as you use the Routines.

- Students who can independently read grade-level words at grade 2 or above do not need additional instruction and practice with phonemic awareness.
- A Screening Routine at the beginning of each phonemic awareness skill strand helps you place students into appropriate Routines.
- Phonemic awareness is about recognizing and manipulating sounds. Linking written words to the Routines as quickly as possible helps students map sounds to print, use the alphabetic principle, and decode and read words with automaticity.
- Students who automatically and successfully perform tasks in the Routines should quickly move to more advanced tasks. The goal is to get to Routines that are challenging in order to provide adequate time to reach proficiency.
- Routines should be used judiciously and expeditiously. Target instruction to meet individual student needs and move students out of the instruction when it is no longer needed.

# Screening Routine: Match Phonemes

Use this Screening Routine to determine entry points for students who may need review or instruction in the skill **matching phonemes.** The Screening Routine should be performed individually.

## SCREENING ROUTINE

### Entry Point 1 Match Phonemes: Initial

I am going to say three words: *cupcake, sidewalk, catnap.* Let's say the first sound in each word. That's right: /k/ *cupcake;* /s/ *sidewalk;* /k/ *catnap.* Now say the two words that have the same beginning sound.

**cupcake /k/**
**sidewalk /s/**
**catnap /k/**

- If students cannot match the initial phonemes in *cupcake* and *catnap,* go to the Routine on p. 5.

### Entry Point 2 Match Phonemes: Final

I am going to say three words: *bookcase, clubhouse, snowman.* Let's say the last sound in each word. That's right: *bookcase* /s/, *clubhouse* /s/, *snowman* /n/. Now say the two words that have the same last sound.

**bookcase /s/**
**clubhouse /s/**
**snowman /n/**

- If students cannot match the final phonemes in *bookcase* and *clubhouse,* go to the Routine on p. 5.

***continued***

*continued*

# Screening Routine: Match Phonemes

## Entry Point 3 Match Phonemes: Medial

I am going to say three words: *houseboat, football, bookshelf.* Listen to the first syllable in each word: *house, foot, book.* Now say the two words that have the same middle sound in the first syllable.

**houseboat** **/ou/**

**football** **/ů/**

**bookshelf** **/ů/**

- If students cannot match the middle phonemes in syllables *foot* and *book,* go to the Routine on p. 5.

## Exit Point

If students can match initial, final, and medial phonemes within syllables, go to the Screening Routine for Isolate Phonemes on p. 7.

**PHONEMIC AWARENESS**
GRADE 3

SIDE A

# Match Phonemes: Initial, Final, and Medial

**Phoneme matching** is the ability to recognize and identify phonemes that are the same in initial, final, or medial positions in words or syllables.

## ROUTINE

### STEP 1 INTRODUCE

Today we will identify the same sounds at the beginning, at the end, and in the middle of words or syllables. Listen as I say the word *man.* The beginning, or initial, sound is /m/; the ending, or final, sound is /n/; and the middle, or medial, sound is /a/.

### STEP 2 MODEL

- Emphasize the initial sound /k/ in *campfire, coattail,* and *cutout.* Let's hold up one finger each time we hear the initial sound /k/ in this sentence.
- Emphasize the final sound /d/ in *bookend, childhood,* and *outside.* Then say: Let's hold up one finger each time we hear the final sound /d/ in this sentence.
- Emphasize the medial sound /e/ in *bedtime, desktop,* and *necklace.* Then say: Let's hold up one finger each time we hear the medial sound /e/ in this sentence.

**The concert started when the conductor came.**

**The bread was homemade.**

**Anya has a velvet sweater.**

### STEP 3 GUIDE PRACTICE

- Listen to these words: *sadness, seaweed, schoolhouse.* Say the initial sound in each word. That's right. It's /s/. Repeat for final and medial phonemes.

**platform, classroom, lonesome** | **milkshake, midnight, sickness**

- **Phonics Connection** Have students write and then read the boxed words.

### STEP 4 ON THEIR OWN

Have students match words that have the same initial, final, or medial phonemes.

**football, forehead, schoolwork** (initial /f/)

**homeroom, nightgown, afternoon** (final /n/)

**clubhouse, moonbeam, sunshine** (medial /u/)

SIDE B

# Match Phonemes: Initial, Final, and Medial

PHONEMIC AWARENESS
GRADE 3

**CORRECTIVE FEEDBACK**

**IF** students cannot match sounds in initial, final, or medial positions,

**THEN** review Steps 2 and 3 and work through the Make It Easier activity.

## Make It Easier

Students who cannot match phonemes may benefit from working with fewer phonemes.

- Listen as I say these words: *pill, pine, pest.* I want you to repeat the sounds with me and listen for the first sound in each word. The sound is /p/. Have students practice with final and medial sounds. Model and assist as needed.
- Practice with these words.

**foot, sit, oat, let, mask, back, pad, flat**

## Make It Harder

Students who can match phonemes in compound words can extend the activity by using multisyllabic words. You may wish to refer to the weekly spelling list to provide words at the student's level.

- Listen as I say these words: *pronounce, pumpkin, paragraph.* What is the initial phoneme in each word? That's right, /p/. Have students practice with final and medial sounds. Model and assist as needed.
- Practice with these words.

**passenger, quarter, scatter, difficult, liquid, miserable**

# Screening Routine: Isolate Phonemes

Use this Screening Routine to determine a student's entry point into the skill **isolate phonemes.** The Screening Routine should be performed individually.

## SCREENING ROUTINE

### Entry Point 1 Isolate Initial Phonemes

I am going to say three words. I want you to listen and say the initial, or first, sound in each word.

**leopard**

**moment**

**interrupt**

- If students cannot identify the initial sounds in *leopard* (/l/), *moment* (/m/), and *interrupt* (/i/), go to the Routine on p. 9.

### Entry Point 2 Isolate Final Phonemes

I am going to say three words. I want you to listen and say the final, or last, sound in each word.

**foolish**

**grumpy**

**scramble**

- If students cannot isolate the final sounds in *foolish* (/sh/), *grumpy* (/ē/), and *scramble,* (/əl/), go to the Routine on p. 11.

***continued***

*continued*

# Screening Routine: Isolate Phonemes

## Entry Point 3 Isolate Medial Phonemes

I am going to say three words. I want you to listen and say the middle sound in the first syllable of each word.

**section**

**happiness**

**townspeople**

- If students cannot isolate the medial sounds in the first syllable of *section* (/e/), *happiness,* (/a/), and *townspeople,* (/ou/), go to the Routine on p. 13.

## Exit Point

If students can isolate initial, final, and medial phonemes, go to the Screening Routine for Blend and Segment Phonemes on p. 15.

**SIDE A**

# Isolate Phonemes: Initial

**Phoneme isolation** is the ability to identify and say a particular phoneme in a word apart from the rest of the word.

## ROUTINE

### STEP 1 INTRODUCE

We can isolate, or separate, sounds at the beginning, in the middle, or at the ends of words to show that we can hear and say each sound. Today we will isolate beginning sounds in words.

### STEP 2 MODEL

- Listen to this word: *goodbye.* Repeat the word slowly, emphasizing each phoneme. Let's isolate the beginning, or initial, sound. The initial sound is /g/. Now say the entire word: *goodbye.* That's right. *Goodbye.*
- Now listen to this word: *overnight.* Repeat the word slowly. What is the initial sound? That's right. The initial sound is /ō/.
- **Phonics Connection** Work with students to write the words *goodbye* and *overnight.* Look at the word *goodbye.* The initial sound in *goodbye* is /g/. What is the letter that represents the sound? That's right. The letter is *g.* Repeat the process for *overnight.*

### STEP 3 GUIDE PRACTICE

- Listen to this word: *customer.* Repeat the word, articulating each sound. Now isolate the initial sound in *customer.* That's right. The initial sound is /k/. Repeat the routine, having students isolate initial sounds in *reporter* and *windowsill.*
- **Phonics Connection** Work with students to write the words *customer, reporter,* and *windowsill.* Which letter spells the initial sound in each of these words: *customer, reporter, windowsill?* Be sure students can identify and isolate the letters *c, r,* and *w* in these words.

### STEP 4 ON THEIR OWN

Have students isolate the initial phonemes in these words and practice writing them.

| | | |
|---|---|---|
| **vacation** (/v/) | **typewriter** (/t/) | **thankful** (/th/) |
| **photograph** (/f/) | **impossible** (/i/) | |

**SIDE B**

# Isolate Phonemes: Initial

## CORRECTIVE FEEDBACK

**IF** students cannot isolate initial phonemes in grade-level words, **THEN** review Steps 2 and 3 and work through the Make It Easier activity.

## Make It Easier

Students who cannot isolate initial phonemes in grade-level words may benefit from working with fewer phonemes.

- I will say a word with four separate sounds. The word is *hiker.* The sounds in *hiker* are /h/ /ī/ /k/ /ėr/. Hold up a finger and say /h/. Hold up another finger and say /ī/. Continue holding up fingers for the remaining sounds. Let's say the word: *hiker.* Now say the first sound. That's right. The first sound is /h/. *Hiker.*
- Practice with these additional words.

| | | |
|---|---|---|
| **smell** (/s/) | **train** (/t/) | **bench** (/b/) |

## Make It Harder

Students who can isolate initial phonemes at the beginnings of words may be ready to focus on writing the words as they associate sound-spelling patterns.

- Listen to this word: *meantime.* What is the initial sound in *meantime?* Yes. The initial sound in *meantime* is /m/. Have students write *meantime.* Be sure they correctly identify the sound-symbol correspondence for the sound /m/ and the letter *m.*
- Continue with the following words. Have students write the words after identifying initial sounds and the letters that spell the sounds.

| | | |
|---|---|---|
| **peaceful** (/p/) | **student** (/s/) | **telescope** (/t/) |

PHONEMIC AWARENESS
GRADE 3

SIDE A

# Isolate Phonemes: Final

**Phoneme isolation** is the ability to identify and say a particular phoneme in a word apart from the rest of the word.

## ROUTINE

### STEP 1 INTRODUCE

We can isolate, or separate, sounds at the beginning, in the middle, or at the ends of words to show that we can hear and say each sound. Today we will isolate sounds at the ends of words.

### STEP 2 MODEL

- Listen to this word: *beneath.* Repeat the word slowly, emphasizing each phoneme: /b/ /ə/ /n/ /ē/ /th/. What is the final sound you hear? That's right. The final sound is /th/. Let's say the entire word together: *beneath.*
- Now listen to this word: *brighten.* Repeat the word slowly: /b/ /r/ /ī/ /t/ /ə/ /n/. What is the final sound? That's right. The final sound is /n/.
- **Phonics Connection** Work with students to write the words *beneath* and *brighten.* Read the words aloud: *beneath, brighten.* Look at the word *beneath.* What are the letters that spell the final sound? That's right. The letters are *th.* Repeat the process for *brighten.*

### STEP 3 GUIDE PRACTICE

- Listen to this word: *buffalo.* Repeat the word slowly: /b/ /u/ /f/ /ə/ /l/ /ō/. Now isolate the final sound in *buffalo.* What is the final sound? That's right. The final sound is /ō/. Repeat the routine, having students isolate the final sound in *ceremony* and *impossible.*
- **Phonics Connection** Have students write the words *buffalo, ceremony,* and *impossible.* Provide help as needed. What is the final sound in each of these words: *buffalo, ceremony,* and *impossible?* Be sure students can isolate the final letters *o, y,* and *le* in these words.

### STEP 4 ON THEIR OWN

Have students isolate the final phonemes in these words and then practice writing them.

| | | |
|---|---|---|
| **otherwise** (/z/) | **Thursday** (/ā/) | **champion** (/n/) |
| **December** (/ėr/) | **government** (/t/) | |

**SIDE B**

# Isolate Phonemes: Final

**CORRECTIVE FEEDBACK**

**IF** students cannot isolate final phonemes in grade-level words,

**THEN** review Steps 2 and 3 and work through the Make It Easier activity.

## Make It Easier

Students who cannot isolate final phonemes in grade-level words may benefit from using fingers to help separate each sound.

- I will say a word with five separate sounds. The word is *approach.* Hold up a finger for each sound. Say: /ə/ /p/ /r/ /ō/ /ch/. Let's say the word: *approach.* Now separate the last sound from the rest of the word. That's right. The last sound is /ch/. *Approach.*
- Practice with these additional words.

| | | |
|---|---|---|
| **insect** (/t/) | **million** (/n/) | **freedom** (/m/) |

## Make It Harder

Students who can isolate final phonemes in grade-level words may be ready to focus on writing the words as they associate sound-spellings.

- Listen to this word: *experience.* What is the final phoneme in *experience?* Yes. The final sound is /s/. Now write the word. Have students write *experience.* Provide guidance as needed.
- Continue with the following words. Have students write the words after identifying the final sounds and letters that spell the sounds.

| | | |
|---|---|---|
| **orchestra** (/ə/) | **introduce** (/s/) | **hummingbird** (/d/) |

SIDE A

# Isolate Phonemes: Medial

**Phoneme isolation** is the ability to identify and say a particular phoneme in a word apart from the rest of the word.

## ROUTINE

### STEP 1 INTRODUCE

We can isolate, or separate, sounds at the beginning, in the middle, or at the ends of words to show that we can hear and say each sound. Today we will isolate sounds in the middle, or medial position, of words or syllables.

### STEP 2 MODEL

- Listen to this word: *candlelight.* There are three syllables in *candlelight: can-dle-light.* The middle sound in the first syllable *can* is /a/. What is the middle sound in the last syllable? The middle sound in *light* is /ī/.
- Now listen to this word: *brownstone: brown-stone.* The middle vowel sound in *brown* is /ou/. What is the middle vowel sound in the last syllable *stone?* That's right. The middle sound is /ō/.
- **Phonics Connection** Work with students to write the words *candlelight* and *brownstone.*

### STEP 3 GUIDE PRACTICE

- Listen to this word: *collection.* Say the syllables with me: *col–lec–tion.* Now isolate the middle sound in the middle syllable of *collection.* The middle sound in the middle syllable is the sound /e/. Repeat the routine, having students isolate the middle vowel sound in the middle syllable of *description* (/i/) and *summarize* (/ə/).
- **Phonics Connection** Have students write the words *collection, description,* and *summarize.* Provide help as needed.

### STEP 4 ON THEIR OWN

Have students isolate the medial phoneme in the first syllable of each word and then write the words.

| | | |
|---|---|---|
| **dictionary** (/i/) | **happiness** (/a/) | **thoughtfulness** (/ȯ/) |
| **mysterious** (/i/) | **peppermint** (/e/) | |

**SIDE B**

# Isolate Phonemes: Medial

**CORRECTIVE FEEDBACK**

| | |
|---|---|
| **IF** students cannot isolate medial phonemes within syllables in grade-level words, | **THEN** review Steps 2 and 3 and work through the Make It Easier activity. |

## Make It Easier

Students who cannot isolate medial phonemes within syllables in grade-level words may benefit from working with words that have fewer phonemes and fewer syllables.

- I will say a word with two syllables. The word is *backward*: *back-ward*. Hold up a finger as you say each syllable. What is the middle sound in the first syllable *back-*? That's right. The middle sound in the first syllable is /a/. *Backward.*
- Practice with these additional words.

| | | |
|---|---|---|
| **lawnmower** (/ȯ/) | **holiday** (/o/) | **whisker** (/i/) |

## Make It Harder

Students who can isolate medial phonemes within syllables in grade-level words may be ready to focus on writing the words as they associate sound-spelling patterns.

- Listen to this word: *community.* What is the middle sound in the first syllable? Yes. The middle sound in the first syllable is /ə/. Now write the word. Have students write *community.* Provide guidance as needed.
- Continue with the following words.

| | | |
|---|---|---|
| **convenience** (/ə/) | **historical** (/i/) | **hummingbird** (/u/) |

# Screening Routine: Blend and Segment Phonemes

Use this Screening Routine to determine a student's entry point into the skill **blend and segment phonemes.** The Screening Routine should be performed individually.

## SCREENING ROUTINE

### Entry Point 1 Blend Phonemes

I am going to say the sounds in a word. I want you to blend the sounds to say the word.

**/k/ /l/ /a/ /p/**

**/t/ /r/ /u/ /ngk/**

**/s/ /t/ /o/ /m/ /p/ /s/**

- If students cannot blend the words *clap, trunk,* and *stomps,* go to the Routine on p. 17.

### Entry Point 2 Segment Phonemes

I am going to say a word. I want you to separate and say each sound in the word.

**place**

**strike**

**planet**

- If students cannot segment the words *place, strike,* and *planet* into /p/ /l/ /ā/ /s/, /s/ /t/ /r/ /ī/ /k/, and /p/ /l/ /a/ /n/ /ə/ /t/, go to the Routine on p. 19.

***continued***

*continued*

# Screening Routine: Blend and Segment Phonemes

## Entry Point 3 Blend and Segment Phonemes

I am going to say a word. I want you to separate and say each sound in the word. Then I want you to blend the sounds together to say the word.

**hand**

**plant**

**napkin**

- If students cannot segment the phonemes /h/ /a/ /n/ /d/ and then blend the word *hand;* /p/ /l/ /a/ /n/ /t/ and then blend the word *plant;* and /n/ /a/ /p/ /k/ /ə/ /n/ and then blend the word *napkin,* go to the Routine on p. 21.

## Exit Point

If students can blend and segment phonemes, go to the Screening Routine for Add and Delete Phonemes on p. 23.

SIDE A

# Blend Phonemes



**Phoneme blending** is the ability to recognize and identify a sequence of spoken sounds and combine them to form a word.

## ROUTINE

### STEP 1 INTRODUCE

Today we will blend, or combine, sounds to form words. We'll focus on words that have five sounds.

### STEP 2 MODEL

- Display five Elkonin boxes. Listen as I blend sounds to say a word. Slide your finger under the boxes as you say the sounds, and then again as you say the word: /a/ /k/ /t/ /i/ /v/. *Active.*

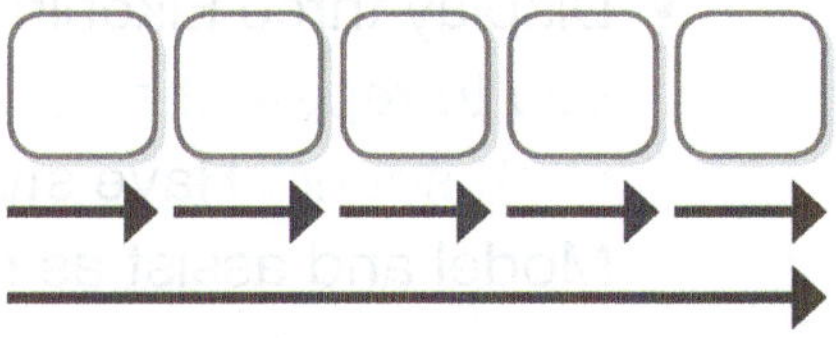

- **Phonics Connection** Write the letters *a, c, t, i, ve* in the Elkonin boxes. Each sound in the word *active* is represented by a letter or letters. I'll blend the sounds again to read the word. Repeat the blending routine, sliding your finger under the boxes containing letters: /a/ /k/ /t/ /i/ /v/. *Active.*

### STEP 3 GUIDE PRACTICE

- Display five Elkonin boxes. Listen as I say these sounds: /a/ /th/ /l/ /ē/ /t/. Now say the sounds with me as we blend the word. Slide your finger under the five boxes as students say the sounds slowly, and then again as they say the word: /a/ /th/ /l/ /ē/ /t/. What is the word? (*athlete*) That is correct. The word is *athlete*.

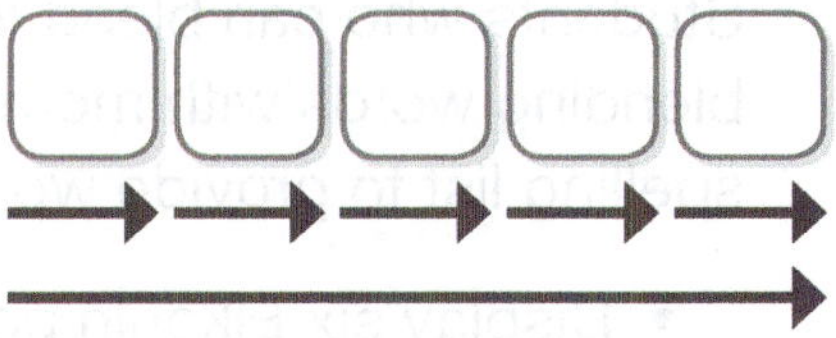

- **Phonics Connection** Write the letters *a, th, l, e, te* in the Elkonin boxes. Have students blend and read the word.

### STEP 4 ON THEIR OWN

Have students blend each word after you say the phonemes.

| | | | | |
|---|---|---|---|---|
| **prepay** | **spooky** | **heroes** | **sample** | **widen** |

SIDE B

# Blend Phonemes

**CORRECTIVE FEEDBACK**

**IF** students cannot blend the sounds of words,

**THEN** model how to blend three- and four-phoneme words, using the Make It Easier activity.

## Make It Easier

Students who cannot blend five-phoneme words may benefit from a more tactile approach using fewer phonemes.

- Display three Elkonin boxes. Listen as I say these sounds: /sh/ /u/ /t/. I want you to repeat the sounds and slide your finger under the boxes as we say each sound. Have students use the Elkonin boxes to blend the sounds. Model and assist as needed.
- Practice with these words.

| | | | | | | |
|---|---|---|---|---|---|---|
| ant | sit | glad | tiny | sand | twin | mask |

## Make It Harder

Students who can blend five-phoneme words can extend the activity by blending words with more phonemes. You may wish to refer to the weekly spelling list to provide words at the student's level.

- Display six Elkonin boxes. Listen as I say these sounds: /k/ /l/ /a/ /s/ /ə/ /z/. I want you to repeat the sounds and slide your finger under the boxes as we say each sound. Have students use Elkonin boxes to blend the sounds and say the word *classes.* Model and assist as needed. Finally, write the letters in the Elkonin boxes and have students blend and read the word. The letters in the boxes should be: *c, l, a, ss, e, s.*
- Practice with these words.

| | | | | | |
|---|---|---|---|---|---|
| basket | maintain | episode | recruit | contrast | citizen |

SIDE A

# Segment Phonemes



**Phoneme segmentation** is the ability to break a word into its individual sounds, or phonemes.

## ROUTINE

### STEP 1 INTRODUCE

Gather five counters. Today we will segment, or break, words into their individual sounds. We'll focus on words that have five sounds.

### STEP 2 MODEL

- Listen to this word: *reason.* I'll clap the number of syllables I hear in *reason.* Clap two times as you say *rea-son.* Then, segment the sounds, placing a counter from left to right as you say each phoneme: /r/ /ē/ /z/ /ə/ /n/. There are five sounds in the word *reason.*

- **Phonics Connection** Each sound in the word *reason* is represented by a letter or letters. I'll say each sound again as I write the word. Segment the word again, writing the letter or letters that represent each sound as you say it: /r/ /ē/ /z/ /ə/ /n/. *Reason.*

r ea s o n

### STEP 3 GUIDE PRACTICE

- Provide students with counters. Clap the syllables in this word: *tasty.* Now say the sounds with me as we segment the word. Have students place counters as they segment the word and say each sound: /t/ /ā/ /s/ /t/ /ē/. How many sounds do we hear? (five)

- **Phonics Connection** Each sound in the word *tasty* is represented by a letter. Let's say the sounds again and write the word. Have students write the word with you: /t/ /ā/ /s/ /t/ /ē/. *Tasty.*

t a s t y

### STEP 4 ON THEIR OWN

Have students tap the syllables and then segment each word using counters. Then have them write the word.

| | | | | |
|---|---|---|---|---|
| blind | outline | master | silence | foolish |

SIDE B

# Segment Phonemes

**CORRECTIVE FEEDBACK**

| | |
|---|---|
| **IF** students cannot segment the sounds of words, | **THEN** model how to segment words with fewer phonemes, using the Make It Easier activity. |

## Make It Easier

Students who cannot segment five-phoneme words may benefit from an approach using fewer phonemes.

- Provide students with counters. Listen as I say this word: *trade.* Now say the sounds with me as we segment the word. Touch a counter as we say each sound. Have students touch counters as they segment the word with you: /t/ /r/ /ā/ /d/. How many sounds do you hear? (four) Model and assist as needed.
- Practice with these words.

| | | | | | | |
|---|---|---|---|---|---|---|
| fail | shrug | grape | stew | clutch | beetle | lace |

## Make It Harder

Students who can segment five-phoneme words can extend the activity by using words with more phonemes. You may wish to refer to the weekly spelling list to provide words at the student's level.

- Listen as I say this word: *kindness.* Now say the sounds with me as we segment the word. Model and assist as needed. Now let's say the sounds again and write the word. Have students write the letter or letters that correspond to each sound as they segment the word *kindness.*
- Practice with these words.

| | | | | |
|---|---|---|---|---|
| sadness | imagine | midnight | treetop | intelligent |

SIDE A

# Segment and Blend Phonemes

**Phoneme segmentation** is the ability to break a word into its individual sounds, or phonemes. **Phoneme blending** is the ability to recognize and identify a sequence of spoken sounds and combine them to form a word.

## ROUTINE

### STEP 1 INTRODUCE

Gather five counters. Today we will segment, or break, words into their individual sounds. Then we will blend, or combine, the sounds to form words. We'll focus on words that have five sounds.

### STEP 2 MODEL

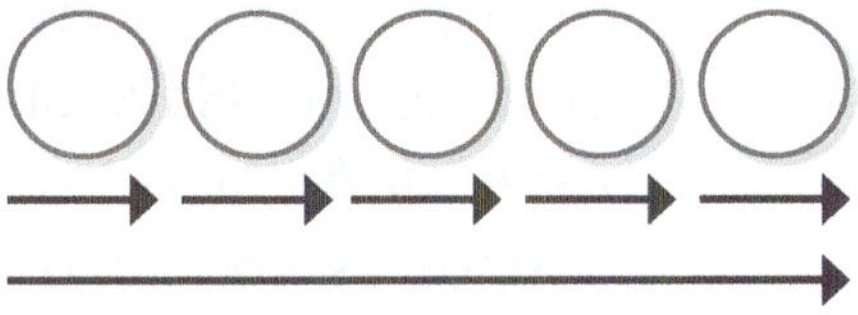

- Place five counters from left to right. Listen to this word: *ticket.* Segment the sounds of the word, touching a counter as you say each phoneme: /t/ /i/ /k/ /ə/ /t/. There are five sounds in the word *ticket.* Now let's blend the sounds. Blend the sounds of the word, sliding a finger under the counters as you say each sound slowly, and then again as you say the word: /t/ /i/ /k/ /ə/ /t/. *Ticket.*

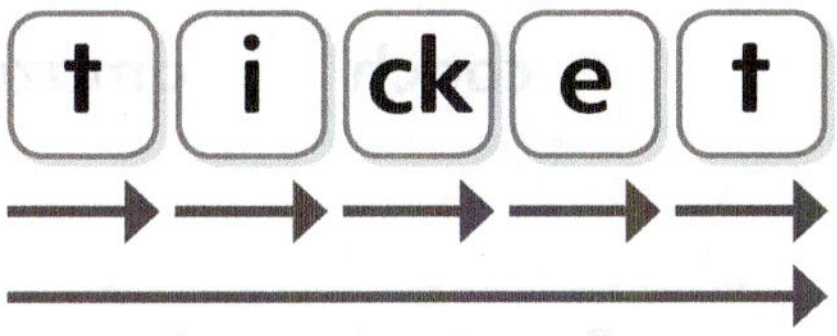


- **Phonics Connection** Each sound in the word *ticket* is represented by a letter or letters. I'll say the sounds again and write the word. Segment the word again, writing the letter or letters that represent each sound as you say it: /t/ /i/ /k/ /ə/ /t/. *Ticket.* Now I'll blend the sounds again to read the word. Slide your finger under the word as you read: /t/ /i/ /k/ /ə/ /t/. *Ticket.*

### STEP 3 GUIDE PRACTICE

- Listen to this word: *marches.* Touch a counter as we say each sound: /m/ /är/ /ch/ /ə/ /z/. Now let's blend the sounds. Have students slide a finger under the counters as they say the word.
- **Phonics Connection** Let's say the sounds again and write the word. Have children segment the word again, writing the letter or letters that represent each sound. Now slide a finger under the letters to blend and read the word.

### STEP 4 ON THEIR OWN

Have students segment and write the word. Then have them blend and read the word.

| | | | | | |
|---|---|---|---|---|---|
| **virus** | **artist** | **mantle** | **rabbit** | **Friday** | **unwrap** |

**SIDE B**

# Segment and Blend Phonemes

**PHONEMIC AWARENESS**
**GRADE 3**

**CORRECTIVE FEEDBACK**

**IF** students cannot segment and blend the sounds of words,

**THEN** model how to segment and blend words with fewer phonemes, using the Make It Easier activity.

## Make It Easier

Students who cannot segment and blend five-phoneme words may benefit from an approach using fewer phonemes.

- Have students place four counters from left to right. Listen as I say this word: *gift.* Now say the sounds with me as we segment the word. Touch a counter as we say each sound. Have students touch the counters as they segment the word with you: /g/ /i/ /f/ /t/. Now we will blend the sounds to say the word. I want you to say the sounds as you slide your finger under the counters. Have students use the counters to blend the sounds. Model and assist as needed.
- Practice with these words.

| | | | | | | |
|---|---|---|---|---|---|---|
| coach | amaze | straw | gold | tooth | shelf | fresh |

## Make It Harder

Students who can segment and blend five-phoneme words can extend the activity by using words with more phonemes and removing the use of counters. You may wish to refer to the weekly spelling list to provide words at the student's level.

- Listen as I say this word: *homework.* I want you to segment the word by saying the sounds. (/h/ /ō/ /m/ /w/ /ėr/ /k/) Now say the sounds again and write the word. Have students write the letter or letters that correspond to each sound as they segment the word *homework.* Finally, have them blend and read the word.
- Practice with these words.

| | | | | | |
|---|---|---|---|---|---|
| helicopter | animal | inventor | frustrated | customer | recycle |

# Screening Routine: Add and Delete Phonemes

Use this Screening Routine to determine a student's entry point into the skill of **phoneme addition and deletion.** The Screening Routine should be performed individually.

## SCREENING ROUTINE

### Entry Point 1 Add Phonemes

I am going to say a word. Then I will say a sound. I want you to add the sound to the word to say a new word.

**art, add /ch/ to the beginning**

- If students cannot say the new word *chart,* go to the Routine on p. 25.

**city, add /z/ to the end**

- If students cannot say the new word *cities,* go to the Routine on p. 27.

**size, add /p/ after /s/**

- If students cannot say the new word *spies,* go to the Routine on p. 29.

### Entry Point 2 Delete Phonemes

I am going to say a word. Then I will say a sound. I want you to delete, or take away, the sound from the word to say a new word.

**bright, take away /b/**

- If students cannot say the new word *right,* go to the Routine on p. 31.

**wait, take away /t/**

- If students cannot say the new word *way,* go to the Routine on p. 33.

**inspect, take away /p/**

- If students cannot say the new word *insect,* go to the Routine on p. 35.

***continued***

*continued*

# Screening Routine: Add and Delete Phonemes

## Exit Point

If students can add and delete phonemes, go to the Screening Routine for Substitute Phonemes on p. 37.

**SIDE A**

# Add Phonemes: Initial

**Phoneme addition** is the ability to say a new word by adding a phoneme (sound) to a word.

## ROUTINE

### STEP 1 INTRODUCE

We can add phonemes, or sounds, to words and make new words. Today we will add sounds to the beginnings of words to make new words.

### STEP 2 MODEL

- Listen to this word: *out.* I will add the beginning sound /p/ to make a new word: /p/ /ou/ /t/, *pout.*
- Now I will add another beginning sound, /s/, to *pout:* /s/ *-pout.* The new word is *spout.*
- Listen again to the word *out.* Now I will add /sh/ at the beginning to make a new word: /sh/ *-out, shout.*
- **Phonics Connection** Write the word *out.* This is the word *out.* Write the letter *p* before *out* to spell *pout.* I can add the sound /p/, represented by the letter *p,* to the beginning of *out.* Run a finger under the word as you blend and read. The new word is *pout.* Write the letter *s* before *pout* to spell *spout.* I added /s/ spelled *s* to spell *spout.*

### STEP 3 GUIDE PRACTICE

- Say this word with me: *rate.* Now add the beginning sound /k/. What new word do we have? (*crate*) Repeat the routine, having students add /ch/ to *air* to make *chair.*
- **Phonics Connection** Have students write the word *air.* To spell the word *chair,* we need to add the sound /ch/ to the beginning of *air.* What letters spell the sound /ch/? Have students add *ch* to spell *chair.*

### STEP 4 ON THEIR OWN

Have students form new words by adding initial phonemes to these words.

| | | | | | |
|---|---|---|---|---|---|
| /sh/ + rug | /k/ + loud | /f/ + east | /s/ + team | /p/ + late | /g/ + ray |

SIDE B

# Add Phonemes: Initial

**CORRECTIVE FEEDBACK**

**IF** students cannot add initial phonemes to form new words,

**THEN** add hand movements, using the Make It Easier activity.

## Make It Easier

Students who cannot say the new word after adding an initial phoneme may benefit from a multisensory approach.

- I will add a sound to a word and say a new word. Hold up one hand and say /p/. Hold up the other hand and say *lay.* Bring your hands together and say *play.* I added /p/ to *lay* to make *play.* Now you try. Have students hold up their hands as they repeat /p/ -*lay, play.*
- Practice with these words.

| | | | | |
|---|---|---|---|---|
| /g/ + lad | /s/ + and | /t/ + win | /m/ + ask | /th/ + ink |

## Make It Harder

Students who can add phonemes at the beginnings of words may be ready to take it a step further by spelling the words.

- Listen to this word: *rice.* What word do you get when you add /p/ to the beginning of *rice?* Write the word. Have students write *price.*
- Continue with the following phonemes and words. Remind students that words that sound the same may not be spelled the same.

| | | |
|---|---|---|
| /s/ + pool (*spool*) | /h/ + old (*hold*) | /g/ + row (*grow*) |
| /s/ + cool (*school*) | /w/ + under (*wonder*) | /sh/ + our (*shower*) |

**PHONEMIC AWARENESS**
GRADE 3

**SIDE A**

# Add Phonemes: Final

**Phoneme addition** is the ability to say a new word by adding a phoneme (sound) to a word.

## ROUTINE

### STEP 1 INTRODUCE

We can add phonemes, or sounds, to words and make new words. Today we will add sounds to the ends of words to make new words.

### STEP 2 MODEL

- Listen to this word: *pain.* I will add the final sound /t/ to make a new word: /p/ /ā/ /n/ /t/, *paint.*
- Now I will add another sound, /s/, to *paint:* /p/ /ā/ /n/ /t/ /s/. The new word is *paints.*
- **Phonics Connection** Write the word *pain.* This is the word *pain.* I can add the sound /t/, represented by the letter *t,* to the end of *pain.* Write the letter *t* after *pain* to spell *paint.* Run a finger under the word as you blend and read. The new word is *paint.* Write the letter *s* after *paint* to spell *paints.* I added /s/ spelled *s* to spell *paints.*

### STEP 3 GUIDE PRACTICE

- Listen to this word: *stay.* Now add the final sound /j/. What new word do we have? (*stage*) Repeat the routine, having students add /ch/ to *tea* to make *teach.*
- **Phonics Connection** Have students write the word *tea.* To spell the word *teach,* we need to add the sound /ch/ to the end of *tea.* What letters spell the sound /ch/? Have students add *ch* to spell *teach.*

### STEP 4 ON THEIR OWN

Have students form new words by adding final phonemes to these words.

| | | |
|---|---|---|
| **store + /m/** (*storm*) | **sun + /ē/** (*sunny*) | **too + /l/** (*tool*) |
| **write + /ėr/** (*writer*) | **travel + /z/** (*travels*) | **tray + /l/** (*trail*) |

SIDE B

# Add Phonemes: Final

## CORRECTIVE FEEDBACK

**IF** students cannot add final phonemes to form new words,

**THEN** repeat Step 3, adding the same final phoneme, /s/, to grade-level words such as *speak, wake, tap, tape, taste, state, tent, test.*

## Make It Easier

Students who cannot say the new word after adding a final phoneme may benefit from a multisensory approach.

- I will add a sound to a word and say a new word. Hold up one hand and say *row.* Hold up the other hand and say /t/. Bring your hands together and say *wrote.* I added /t/ to *row* to make *wrote.* Now you try. Have students hold up their hands as they repeat *row-* /t/, *wrote.*
- Practice with these words.

| | | |
|---|---|---|
| **zoo + /m/** (*zoom*) | **we + /k/** (*week*) | **notebook + /s/** (*notebooks*) |
| **way + /v/** (*wave*) | **scar + /f/** (*scarf*) | **allow + /d/** (*aloud*) |

## Make It Harder

Students who can add phonemes at the ends of words may be ready to take it a step further by spelling the words.

- Listen to this word: *fell.* What word do you get when you add /ō/ to the end of *fell?* Write the word. Have students write *fellow.*
- Continue with the following words and phonemes.

| | | |
|---|---|---|
| **beet + /əl/** (*beetle*) | **meal + /z/** (*meals*) | **eight + /ē/** (*eighty*) |
| **for + /s/** (*force*) | **hand + /əl/** (*handle*) | **her + /d/** (*herd*) |

SIDE A

# Add Phonemes: Within Words

**Phoneme addition** is the ability to say a new word by adding a phoneme (sound) to a word.

## ROUTINE

### STEP 1 INTRODUCE

We can add phonemes, or sounds, to words and make new words. Today we will add sounds within words to make new words.

### STEP 2 MODEL

- Listen to this word: *tickle.* I will add the sound /r/ after /t/ to make a new word: /t/ /r/ /i/ /k/ /əl/, *trickle.*
- **Phonics Connection** Write the word *tickle.* This is the word *tickle.* Write the word *trickle* under *tickle* and underline the *r.* I can add the sound /r/, represented by the letter *r,* after the *t* in *tickle* to spell a new word. Run a finger under the word as you blend and read. The new word is *trickle.*

### STEP 3 GUIDE PRACTICE

- Listen to this word: *sash.* Now add the sound /m/ after /s/. What new word do we have? (*smash*) Repeat the routine, having students add /n/ after /m/ /u/ in *much* to make *munch*.
- **Phonics Connection** Have students write the word *much.* To spell the word *munch,* we need to add the sound /n/ spelled *n* within the word. Where will you add an *n?* Have students write the new word *munch.*

### STEP 4 ON THEIR OWN

Have students form new words by adding phonemes within these words.

| | | |
|---|---|---|
| **matter/master** (/s/) | **male/maple** (/p/) | **lighting/lightning** (/n/) |
| **quit/quilt** (/l/) | **sale/scale** (/k/) | |

**SIDE B**

# Add Phonemes: Within Words

### CORRECTIVE FEEDBACK

| | |
|---|---|
| **IF** students cannot add phonemes within words to form new words, | **THEN** model the correct responses, repeating Steps 2 and 3. |

## Make It Easier

Students who cannot add a phoneme within a word and say the new word may need additional practice segmenting sounds.

- Hold up a finger as you say each sound in the word *seem.* /s/ /ē/ /m/. There are three sounds in the word *seem.* Using your other hand, hold up a finger as you say each sound in the word *steam:* /s/ /t/ /ē/ /m/. There are four sounds in the word *steam.* I added the sound /t/ to *seem* to make *steam.* Now you try. Have students segment the sounds in *seem* on one hand and the sounds in *steam* on the other hand.
- Practice with these words.

| | | |
|---|---|---|
| **bed/bread** | **cab/crab** | **sash/smash** |
| **seal/steal** | **stain/strain** | **seek/sneak** |

## Make It Harder

Students who can add phonemes within words may be ready to take it a step further by spelling the words.

- Listen to this word: *say.* What word do you get when you add /w/ after /s/ in *say?* Write the word. Have students write *sway.* Then write the word on the board and have students compare.
- Continue with the following words and phonemes.

| | | |
|---|---|---|
| **tile/title** (/t/) | **shed/shred** (/r/) | **sun/spun** (/p/) |
| **couch/crouch** (/r/) | **soup/swoop** (/w/) | |

**SIDE A**

# Delete Phonemes: Initial

**Phoneme deletion** is the ability to say the word that remains when a specific phoneme is removed.

## ROUTINE

### STEP 1 INTRODUCE

We can delete, or take away, sounds from words to make new words. Today we will take away sounds from the beginnings of words.

### STEP 2 MODEL

- Listen to this word: *strap.* I will take away the beginning sound /s/ to make a new word. *Strap* without /s/ is *trap.*
- **Phonics Connection** Write the word *strap.* This is the word *strap.* Erase the letter *s* at the beginning of the word to spell *trap.* I can take away the sound /s/, represented by the letter *s,* from the beginning of *strap.* Run a finger under the word as you blend and read. The new word is *trap.*

### STEP 3 GUIDE PRACTICE

- Say this word with me: *thread.* Now take away the beginning sound /th/. What new word do we have? (*red*) Repeat the routine, having students delete the first phoneme from *groom, drank,* and *yearn.*
- **Phonics Connection** Have students write the word *yearn.* The first sound in *yearn* is /y/, spelled *y.* Have students cover the *y* in the word *yearn.* What word do you have now? Have students write the word *earn* under *yearn.*

### STEP 4 ON THEIR OWN

Have students form new words by deleting initial phonemes from these words.

| | | |
|---|---|---|
| lice - /l/ | loyal - /l/ | sleep - /s/ |
| adore - /ə/ | cash - /k/ | crinkle - /k/ |

SIDE B

# Delete Phonemes: Initial

## CORRECTIVE FEEDBACK

**IF** students cannot delete initial phonemes, | **THEN** add hand movements, using the Make It Easier activity.

## Make It Easier

Students who cannot say the new word after deleting the initial phoneme may benefit from a multisensory approach.

- I will take away the first sound from a word and say a new word. Hold up both hands, palms facing students, and say *drip*. Bounce your right hand as you say /d/, then bounce your left hand as you say /rip/. We can take away the first sound, /d/. What is left? Bounce your left hand as you say /rip/.
- Practice with these words.

| | | |
|---|---|---|
| **dare - /d/** | **charm - /ch/** | **arose - /ə/** |
| **freight - /f/** | **oyster - /oi/** | |

## Make It Harder

Students who can delete initial phonemes may be ready to delete more than one phoneme and discuss the difference in word meanings.

- Listen to this word: *uncover.* What word do you get when you take away /un/ from *uncover?* (*cover*) To *cover* is to place something over something else. To *uncover* is the opposite. It means "to take something off."
- Continue with the following phonemes and words.

| | | |
|---|---|---|
| **uncomfortable - /un/** | **disagree - /dis/** | **react - /rē/** |
| **disappear - /dis/** | **misunderstand - /mis/** | **impossible - /im/** |
| **impatient - /im/** | | |

SIDE A

# Delete Phonemes: Final

**Phoneme deletion** is the ability to say the word that remains when a specific phoneme is removed.

## ROUTINE

### STEP 1 INTRODUCE

We can delete, or take away, sounds from words to make new words. Today we will take away sounds from the ends of words.

### STEP 2 MODEL

- Listen to this word: *mourn.* I will take away the final sound /n/ to make a new word. *Mourn* without the final /n/ is *more.*
- **Phonics Connection** Write the word *mourn.* This is the word *mourn.* When I take away the sound /n/, the new word is *more.* Write the word *more* under *mourn,* then point to the *n* at the end of *mourn.* The sound /n/, represented by the letter *n,* is in the word *mourn.* But it is not in the word *more.* That's not all that is different about these words. Sometimes when we take away a sound from a word, the spelling of the word changes in other ways. Run a finger under the words as you blend and read them again.

### STEP 3 GUIDE PRACTICE

- Say this word with me: *plump.* Now take away the final sound /p/. What new word do we have? (*plum*) Repeat the routine, having students delete the final phoneme from *mild, napkins,* and *knead.*
- **Phonics Connection** Have students write the word *plump.* The final sound in *plump* is /p/, spelled *p.* Have students cover the *p* at the end of the word *plump.* What word do you have now? Have students write the word *plum* under *plump.*

### STEP 4 ON THEIR OWN

Have students form new words by deleting final phonemes from these words.

| | | |
|---|---|---|
| manner - /ėr/ | source - /s/ | heal - /l/ |
| cubes - /z/ | fort - /t/ | beginner - /ėr/ |

SIDE B

# Delete Phonemes: Final

**CORRECTIVE FEEDBACK**

**IF** students cannot delete final phonemes to form new words,

**THEN** repeat Step 3, removing the same final phoneme, /z/, from grade-level words such as *speakers, ruffles, printers, threads, settles, requires.*

## Make It Easier

Students who cannot say the new word after deleting a final phoneme may need more explicit instruction in segmenting sounds.

- Listen to this word: *dome.* Hold out one hand and make a chopping motion moving from left to right as you say each sound. Let's segment the sounds in *dome:* /d/ /ō/ /m/. Now we will say the word without /m/. Repeat the chopping motions as you say the new word: /d/ /ō/. We took away /m/ from *dome* to make *dough.* Now you try. Have students make chopping motions as they segment /d/ /ō/ /m/ and then /d/ /ō/.
- Practice with these words.

| | | |
|---|---|---|
| **troop - /p/** | **stale - /l/** | **willow - /ō/** |
| **bridle - /əl/** | **blurt - /t/** | **daze - /z/** |

## Make It Harder

Students who can delete phonemes at the ends of words should work on the following extension activity.

- Have students work in pairs. One student should say a word.
- The other student should say the word without the final phoneme. Tell students that the new word might be a silly word.
- If the new word is a word they know, they should write the word pair. Then have students share their lists.

**SIDE A**

# Delete Phonemes: Within Words

**Phoneme deletion** is the ability to say the word that remains when a specific phoneme is removed.

## ROUTINE

### STEP 1 INTRODUCE

We can delete, or take away, sounds from words to make new words. Today we will take away sounds from within words.

### STEP 2 MODEL

- Listen to this word: *blend.* I will take away the sound /l/ to make a new word. *Blend* without /l/ is *bend.*
- **Phonics Connection** Write the word *blend.* This is the word *blend.* Erase the letter *l.* I can take away the sound /l/, represented by the letter *l,* from the word *blend.* Run a finger under the word as you blend and read. The new word is *bend.*

### STEP 3 GUIDE PRACTICE

- Say this word with me: *crouch.* Now take away the sound /r/. What new word do we have? (*couch*) Repeat the routine, having students delete the sound /s/ from *roost,* the sound /t/ from *steak,* and /p/ from *spur.*
- **Phonics Connection** Have students write the word *crouch.* We can take away the letter *r* to spell a new word. What word do we get when we take away the *r*? Write it. Students should write the word *couch.*

### STEP 4 ON THEIR OWN

Have students form new words by deleting phonemes from these words.

| | | |
|---|---|---|
| scat - /k/ | scour - /k/ | speller - /p/ |
| vest - /s/ | plaster - /s/ | sent - /n/ |

SIDE B

# Delete Phonemes: Within Words

**CORRECTIVE FEEDBACK**

| | |
|---|---|
| **IF** students cannot delete phonemes within words to form new words, | **THEN** model the correct response, repeating Steps 2 and 3. |

## Make It Easier

Students who cannot say the new word after deleting a phoneme within the word may need more explicit instruction in segmenting sounds.

- Listen to this word: *frill.* How many sounds do we hear in *frill?* Hold up a finger as you say each sound: /f/ /r/ /i/ /l/. There are four sounds in *frill.* Continue to hold up four fingers. Now let's say *frill* without the sound /r/. Touch a finger as you say each sound, skipping the second finger that corresponds to /r/: /f/ /i/ /l/. We took away /r/ from *frill* to make *fill.* Now you try. Have students hold up fingers as they segment /f/ /r/ /i/ /l/ and then /f/ /i/ /l/.
- Practice with these words.

| | | |
|---|---|---|
| grasp - /r/ | stale - /t/ | sport - /p/ |
| dandy - /n/ | skip - /k/ | sweat - /w/ |

## Make It Harder

Students who can delete phonemes within words should work on the following extension activity.

- Listen to the following words. Tell me what new word you can make by deleting a sound from within the word.

| | | | | | |
|---|---|---|---|---|---|
| spun | silk | pinch | task | split | snack |
| smash | munch | limp | mist | pest | |

- You may also have teams work together to write the new words.

# Screening Routine: Substitute Phonemes

Use this Screening Routine to determine entry points for students who may need review or instruction in the skill **substitute phonemes,** a part of **phoneme manipulation.** The Screening Routine should be performed individually.

## SCREENING ROUTINE

### Entry Point 1 Substitute Initial Phonemes

Listen carefully as I say a word. I will ask you to change one sound in the word. Then you will say the new word.

***port:* change /p/ to /sh/. What is the new word?** (*short*)

***black:* change /b/ to /s/. What is the new word?** (*slack*)

***whistle:* change /wh/ to /th/. What is the new word?** (*thistle*)

***boulder:* change /b/ to /sh/. What is the new word?** (*shoulder*)

- If students cannot substitute initial phonemes, go to the Routine on p. 39.

### Entry Point 2 Substitute Final Phonemes

Listen carefully as I say a word. I will ask you to change one part of the word. Then you will say the new word.

***skull:* change /l/ to /ngk/. What is the new word?** (*skunk*)

***send:* change /d/ to /t/. What is the new word?** (*sent*)

***helpful:* change *-ful* to *-ers.* What is the new word?** (*helpers*)

- If students cannot substitute final phonemes, go to the Routine on p. 41.

***continued***

*continued*

# Screening Routine: Substitute Phonemes

## Entry Point 3 Substitute Medial Phonemes

Listen carefully as I say a word. I will ask you to change one sound in the word. Then you will say the new word.

***shell:* change /e/ to /ȯ/. What is the new word?** (*shawl*)

***buggy:* change /u/ to /a/. What is the new word?** (*baggy*)

***carton:* Change /ə/ to /ü/. What is the new word?** (*cartoon*)

- If students cannot manipulate the middle sounds in words or syllables, use the Routine on p. 43.

## Exit Point

If students can identify and substitute initial, final, and medial sounds in words and syllables, go to the Screening Routine for Chain and Reverse Phonemes on p. 49.

**SIDE A**

# Substitute Initial Phonemes

**Initial phoneme substitution** is the ability to change sounds at the beginnings of words or syllables. It is part of **phoneme manipulation.** Knowing how to substitute initial phonemes helps readers learn to decode unfamiliar words.

## ROUTINE

### STEP 1 INTRODUCE

We can substitute, or change, sounds at the beginning, in the middle, or at the ends of words or syllables to show that we can hear and say different word parts. Today we will substitute sounds at the beginning of words.

### STEP 2 MODEL

- Listen to this word: *fearful.* The initial sound is /f/. I'm going to change the sound /f/ to /t/. What is the new word? That's right. The new word is *tearful.*
- Now listen to this word: *buckle.* Let's change the initial sound /b/ to /ch/. What is the new word? Yes—*buckle* becomes *chuckle.*
- Listen to this word: *trail.* Let's change the first sound in the blend /tr/ to /f/. The blend becomes /fr/. What is the new word? That's right. It's *frail.*
- **Phonics Connection** Work with students to say and then write word pairs *fearful/tearful; buckle/chuckle; trail/frail.* Help them make connections between sounds and letters.

### STEP 3 GUIDE PRACTICE

- Listen to this word: *doodle.* Change the first sound /d/ to /p/. What's the new word? It's *poodle.* Have students change *creatures* to *bleachers.*
- **Phonics Connection** Help students recognize that words that sound the same may not be spelled the same, even if only their initial sound changes. Work with them to write *creatures* and *bleachers.* Emphasize sound-symbol correspondences.

### STEP 4 ON THEIR OWN

Have students manipulate initial sounds in the pairs and write the words.

**dancer** → **prancer**　　**measure** → **pleasure**

**shimmer** → **dimmer**

**SIDE B**

# Substitute Initial Phonemes

**CORRECTIVE FEEDBACK**

**IF** students cannot substitute initial sounds in words or syllables,

**THEN** review Steps 2 and 3 and work through the Make It Easier activity.

## Make It Easier

Students who cannot substitute initial phonemes in grade-level words may benefit from reviewing phonemes in words with fewer sounds.

- Listen to this word: *cream.* Hold up a finger for each phoneme as you say the word again slowly: /k/ /r/ /ē/ /m/. Let's say the word together: *cream.* Now let's change the first blend in the word. Let's change /kr/ to /dr/. Listen to the sounds: /d/ /r/ /ē/ /m/. What's the word? That's right. It's *dream.*
- Practice with these additional words.

slate → plate　clip → slip　train → brain

## Make It Harder

Students who can substitute initial phonemes at the beginnings of grade-level words may be ready to focus on spelling differences in words with similar sounds.

- Listen to this word: *farewell—fare-well.* What is the initial sound in *farewell? Yes.* The initial sound is /f/. Now change the sound /f/ to the blend /st/. What is the word? The word is *stairwell.* Let's write the words. Guide students to recognize that the spelling of the *r*-controlled vowel changes, though the sound is the same.
- Continue with the following word pairs. Have students write the words after substituting initial sounds. Discuss spelling differences in the words when the initial sound changes.

foolish → ghoulish　bubble → trouble

candle → sandal

PHONEMIC AWARENESS
GRADE 3

SIDE A

# Substitute Final Phonemes

**Final phoneme substitution** is the ability to change sounds at the ends of words or syllables. It is part of **phoneme manipulation.** Knowing how to substitute final phonemes helps readers decode unfamiliar words.

## ROUTINE

### STEP 1 INTRODUCE

We can substitute, or change, sounds at the beginning, in the middle, or at the ends of words or syllables to make different words. Today we will substitute final sounds in words.

### STEP 2 MODEL

- Listen to this word: *count.* Let's change the final blend /nt/ to the digraph /ch/. What is the new word? That's right. The new word is *couch.*
- Now listen to this word: *bold.* Let's change the final blend from /ld/ to /lt/. What is the new word? Yes—*bold* becomes *bolt.*
- Listen to this word: *summary.* Stretch out the syllables: *sum-mar-y.* Change the final letter *-y* to the letters *-ize.* What is the new word? That's right. It's *summarize.* By changing the ending, I've changed a noun to a verb.
- **Phonics Connection** Have students say and write word pairs *count/couch, bold/bolt,* and *summary/summarize.* Emphasize sound-symbol correspondences.

### STEP 3 GUIDE PRACTICE

- Listen to this word: *respectful.* Separate the syllables: *re-spect-ful.* Change the final syllable *-ful* to *-able.* What's the new word? Yes. It's *respectable.*
- **Phonics Connection** Help students understand that changing suffixes can change the meanings of words. Work with them to write *respectful* and *respectable.*

### STEP 4 ON THEIR OWN

Have students substitute the endings in the first word of each pair to create the second word. Then have students write the words.

| | | | |
|---|---|---|---|
| **medical** → | **medication** | **library** → | **librarian** |
| **symphony** → | **symphonic** | | |

SIDE B

# Substitute Final Phonemes

**CORRECTIVE FEEDBACK**

| | |
|---|---|
| **IF** students cannot substitute final sounds in grade-level words or syllables, | **THEN** review Steps 2 and 3 and work through the Make It Easier activity. |

## Make It Easier

Students who cannot substitute final sounds in grade-level words may benefit from working with fewer phonemes.

- Listen to this word: *tool.* Hold up a finger for each phoneme as you say the word again slowly: /t/ /ü/ /l/. Let's say the word together: *tool.* Now let's change the last sound in the word. Let's change /l/ to /th/. Listen to the sounds: /t/ /ü/ /th/. What's the word? That's right. It's *tooth.*
- Practice with these additional words.

luck → lump
mush → much
maid → main

## Make It Harder

Students who can substitute final phonemes at the ends of words may be ready to focus on sound-spelling differences in manipulated words.

- Listen to this word: *volcano.* Repeat the word slowly, emphasizing each syllable: *vol-ca-no.* What is the final sound in *volcano? Yes.* The final sound is /ō/. Now change the sound /ō/ to the sounds /i/ /k/. What is the word? That's right. The word is *volcanic.* Let's say and write the words. Guide students to recognize that sometimes when a final sound changes, the vowel sound can also change.
- Continue with the following words. Have students write the words after substituting final sounds. Discuss sound-spelling correspondences.

pint → pinch
chant → change
grape → graph

PHONEMIC AWARENESS
GRADE 3

SIDE A

# Substitute Medial Phonemes

**Medial phoneme substitution** is the ability to change sounds within words or syllables. It is part of **phoneme manipulation.** Knowing how to substitute phonemes helps readers decode unfamiliar words.

## ROUTINE

### STEP 1 INTRODUCE

We can substitute, or change, sounds at the beginning, in the middle, or at the ends of words or syllables to make different words. Today we will substitute middle, or medial, sounds.

### STEP 2 MODEL

- Listen to this word: *grave.* Let's change the middle vowel sound /ā/ to the vowel sound /ü/. What is the new word? Yes. It's *groove.*
- Now listen to this word: *daze.* Let's change the middle vowel sound from /ā/ to /ō/. What is the new word? Yes—*daze* becomes *doze.*
- Listen to this word: *grief.* Change the middle vowel sound /ē/ to /a/. What is the new word? That's right. It's *graph.*
- **Phonics Connection** Work with students to say and then write word pairs *grave/groove; daze/doze; grief/graph.* Help them recognize sound-symbol correspondences.

### STEP 3 GUIDE PRACTICE

- Listen to this word: *sort.* Now change the middle sound /ôr/ to /ö/. What's the new word? That's right. It's *sought.*
- Listen to this word: *safer.* Now change the middle sound in the first syllable from /ā/ to /u/. What's the new word? Yes. It's *suffer.*
- **Phonics Connection** Help students say and write the word pairs *sort/sought* and *safer/suffer.* Discuss sound-symbol correspondences.

### STEP 4 ON THEIR OWN

Have students substitute medial sounds in the first word of each pair to create the second word. Then have students write the words.

**spool** → **spoil**     **study** → **sturdy**

**trapper** → **trouper**

PHONEMIC AWARENESS
GRADE 3

SIDE B

# Substitute Medial Phonemes

**CORRECTIVE FEEDBACK**

| | |
|---|---|
| **IF** students cannot substitute medial sounds in words or syllables, | **THEN** review Steps 2 and 3 and work through the Make It Easier activity. |

## Make It Easier

Students who cannot substitute medial sounds in grade-level words may benefit from working with fewer phonemes.

- Listen to this word: *bat.* Let's say the word together: *bat.* Now let's change the middle sound in the word. Let's change /a/ to /ȯ/. Listen to the sounds: /b/ /ȯ/ /t/. What's the word? That's right. It's *bought.*
- Practice with these additional words.

lack → luck

cross → crease

broth → breath

## Make It Harder

Students who can substitute medial phonemes within words may be ready to focus on sound-symbol differences in manipulated words.

- Listen to this word: *cuff.* What is the middle sound in *cuff?* Yes. The middle sound is /u/. Now change the sound /u/ to /ȯ/. What is the word? The word is *cough.* Let's say and write the words. Guide students to recognize sound-symbol differences.
- Continue with the following words. Have students write the words after manipulating medial sounds. Discuss sound-symbol correspondences.

bruise → browse

bless → blouse

dairy → diary

SIDE A

# Substitute Syllables

**Syllable substitution** is the ability to change word parts in multisyllabic words. It is part of **phoneme manipulation.** Substituting syllables helps readers learn how word parts work.

## ROUTINE

### STEP 1 INTRODUCE

Syllables are word parts that contain one vowel sound. When we substitute, or change, syllables at the beginning, in the middle, or at the ends of words, we form different words. Today we will substitute syllables in all word positions.

### STEP 2 MODEL

- Listen to this word: *aside.* I'm going to change the beginning syllable *a-* to the syllable *out-*. The new word is *outside. Aside* means "to the side, or apart"; *outside* means "on the outer part of something."
- Now listen to this word: *childhood.* Let's change the final syllable *-hood to -proof.* What is the new word? Yes—*childhood* becomes *childproof. Childhood* means "the state of being a child," whereas *childproof* means "designed to stop children from injury."
- Listen to this word: *attention.* Let's change the middle syllable from *-ten-* to *-trac-.* What is the new word? It's *attraction.* Discuss meaning changes.
- **Phonics Connection** Work with students to say and then write each word pair.

### STEP 3 GUIDE PRACTICE

- Listen to this word: *behave.* Change the last syllable *-have* to *-hind.* What's the new word? That's right. It's *behind.* Discuss meanings.
- Listen to this word: *refuse.* Changer the first syllable from *re-* to *con-.* What's the new word? *Confuse.* Discuss meaning changes in the two words.
- Listen to this word: *paragraph.* Change both the first and middle syllables from *par-a-* to *phon-o-*. What's the new word? The word is now *phonograph.*
- **Phonics Connection** Help students say and write the word pairs.

### STEP 4 ON THEIR OWN

Have students substitute syllables to change the first word to the second. Then have them write the words and discuss sound-symbol correspondences.

**cardboard** → **chalkboard**  **invention** → **infection**

SIDE B

# Substitute Syllables

## CORRECTIVE FEEDBACK

| | |
|---|---|
| **IF** students cannot substitute syllables in grade-level words, | **THEN** review Steps 2 and 3 and work through the Make It Easier activity. |

## Make It Easier

Students who cannot substitute syllables in grade-level words may benefit from working with words with fewer syllables.

- Listen to this word: *darken.* Say the two syllables slowly: *dark-en.* Let's say the word together: *darken.* Now let's substitute the first syllable *dark-* with the syllable *black-.* What's the new word? That's right. It's *blacken.*
- Practice with these additional words.

| | | | | |
|---|---|---|---|---|
| **forward** → **backward** | **doorstep** → **doorstop** |
| **explorer** → **expander** | |

## Make It Harder

Ask students to change the first word in each pair to the second by directing them to change one syllable. Then have them pick one of the pairs and write sentences for both words.

| | |
|---|---|
| **medicine** → **medicate** | **comfortable** → **compostable** |
| **deliver** → **deceiver** | |

PHONEMIC AWARENESS
GRADE 3

SIDE A

# Substitute Affixes

**Affix substitution** is the ability to change prefixes or suffixes in words. Knowing how to substitute affixes helps readers learn to decode unfamiliar words.

## ROUTINE

### STEP 1 INTRODUCE

We can substitute, or change, affixes in words to make different words. Today we will substitute prefixes and suffixes in words.

### STEP 2 MODEL

- Listen to this word: *uncover.* I can change the prefix *un-* to *re-*. The new word is *recover.*
- Listen to this word: *attention.* I can change the final suffix from *-tion* to *-tive.* The new word is *attentive.*
- **Phonics Connection** Write the word pairs above. Discuss how the spellings, parts of speech, and word meanings have changed.

### STEP 3 GUIDE PRACTICE

- Listen to this word: *thoughtful.* Now change the final suffix *-ful* to *-less.* What's the new word? (*thoughtless*)
- **Phonics Connection** Have students write the words above. Help them recognize that changing affixes can change the spellings, meanings, and parts of speech of a word.

### STEP 4 ON THEIR OWN

Have students substitute the affixes in the first word of each pair to create the second word. Students then write the words and discuss how pronunciations, meanings, and parts of speech can change when affixes change.

**require** → **inquire** | **distract** → **retract**
**approve** → **disprove**

SIDE B

# Substitute Affixes

**CORRECTIVE FEEDBACK**

| | |
|---|---|
| **IF** students cannot substitute affixes in grade-level words, | **THEN** review Steps 2 and 3 and work through the Make It Easier activity. |

## Make It Easier

Students who cannot substitute affixes in grade-level words may benefit by breaking the routine into two parts.

- Listen to this word: *unload.* Now let's take away the prefix *un-* from the word. What's the word? That's right. It's *load.*
- Now add the prefix *re-* before *load*. What's the word? (*reload*)
- Practice with these additional words.

| | | | | | |
|---|---|---|---|---|---|
| **rehearsal** | → | **rehearsing** | **sharpener** | → | **sharpening** |
| **enclose** | → | **disclose** | | | |

## Make It Harder

Students who can substitute affixes may be ready to create multiple new words using different affixes.

- Listen to this word: *admire.* Can you think of any prefixes or suffixes that we can add onto the word *admire* to create a new word? (*admired, admiring, admiration, admires, admirable, unadmirable*)
- Continue with the following words. Have students write the words after substituting affixes. Discuss how the spellings, parts of speech, and meanings have changed.

| | | |
|---|---|---|
| **produce** | → | **reduce, production, producing, produced, introduce** |
| **publish** | → | **published, publisher, publishing, republish, publishable** |
| **imagine** | → | **imagined, imaginative, imagining, unimaginative, imagines** |

# Screening Routine: Chain and Reverse Phonemes

Use this Screening Routine to determine a student's entry point into the skills of **phoneme chaining and reversal.** The Screening Routine should be performed individually.

## SCREENING ROUTINE

### Entry Point 1 Chain Phonemes

I am going to say a word. Then I will ask you to add, delete, or change a sound. I want you to tell me the new word.

**cable,** take away /k/ (*able*)
**able,** add /st/ to the beginning (*stable*)
**stable,** change /ā/ to /u/ (*stubble*)
**stubble,** change /st/ to /b/ (*bubble*)
**bubble,** add /z/ to the end (*bubbles*)

- If students cannot make a word chain by adding, deleting, and substituting the sounds, go to the Routine for Phoneme Chaining on p. 51.

### Entry Point 2 Reverse Phonemes

I am going to say a word. I want you to say the sounds of the word backward to make a new word.

**peach** (*cheap*)
**lime** (*mile*)
**save** (*vase*)

- If students cannot reverse phonemes to say a new word, use the Routine for Phoneme Reversal on p. 53.

***continued***

*continued*

# Screening Routine: Chain and Reverse Phonemes

## Exit Point

If students can chain and reverse phonemes, transition them out of the Phonemic Awareness Routines and into other areas of instruction where they may need support.

SIDE A

# Chain Phonemes

**Phoneme chaining,** a part of **phoneme manipulation,** is an exercise in which one sound is changed to make each new word in a list of words. Sounds might be added, deleted, substituted, or resequenced.

## ROUTINE

### STEP 1 INTRODUCE

We can manipulate, or change, sounds at the beginning, in the middle, or at the end of a word to create new words. Today we will manipulate the sounds in a word to create new words.

### STEP 2 MODEL

- Listen to this word: *pry.* I can add /d/ to the end of the word. The new word is *pride.* I will change the ending sound /d/ to /z/. The new word is *prize.* Now I will change the vowel sound in *prize* from /ī/ to /ā/: *praise.* I can change the beginning sound /p/ to /gr/. The new word is *graze.* I will take /r/ out of *graze.* The new word is *gaze.*
- **Phonics Connection** Write *pry.* This is the word *pry.* In *pry,* /ī/ is spelled *y.* Write *pride* under *pry.* This is the word *pride.* In the word *pride,* /ī/ is spelled *i,* consonant, *e.* When I add /d/ at the end of the word, the spelling of the sound /ī/ changes. Continue with other words in the chain. Discuss the spelling of each word and how it has changed.

**pry**
**pride**
**prize**
**praise**
**graze**
**gaze**

### STEP 3 GUIDE PRACTICE

- Listen to this word: *tea.* Let's add /m/ to the end of the word. What's the word? (*team*) Change /m/ to /ch/. What's the word? (*teach*) Change /t/ to /p/. What's the word? (*peach*) Change the /ē/ to /ou/. What's the word now? (*pouch*) Take away /p/. What's the word? (*ouch*)
- **Phonics Connection** Write the word *tea.* To write the word *team,* we need to add /m/ to the end of the word. Write *team* under the word *tea.* Continue with the words *teach, peach, pouch,* and *ouch* to create a word chain. Discuss the spelling of each word and how it has changed.

**tea**
**team**
**teach**
**peach**
**pouch**
**ouch**

### STEP 4 ON THEIR OWN

Listen to this word: *slither.* Change /th/ to /v/. What's the word? (*sliver*) Now take away the /s/. What's the word? (*liver*) Now change /v/ to /t/. What's the word? (*litter*) Now add /d/ at the end of the word. What's the word? (*littered*)

**SIDE B**

# Chain Phonemes

### CORRECTIVE FEEDBACK

| | |
|---|---|
| **IF** students cannot manipulate phonemes and graphemes to create a word chain, | **THEN** work through the Make It Easier activity and review Steps 2 and 3 if needed. |

## Make It Easier

Students who cannot manipulate phonemes in grade-level words may practice identifying which sounds have changed in different words in a sound chain.

- Listen to these words: *braid, brain.* There is one sound that is different in these words. Tap the sounds with your finger. Listen as I segment the sounds: /b/ /r/ /ā/ /d/; /b/ /r/ /ā/ /n/. Which sound is different? (/d/ changed to /n/) Listen to these words: *brain, train.* /b/ /r/ /ā/ /n/; /t/ /r/ /ā/ /n/. Which sound is different? (/b/ changed to /t/) Now listen to these words: *train, rain.* /t/ /r/ /ā/ /n/; /r/ /ā/ /n/. Which sound is different? (/t/ *was deleted*)
- Continue with the word chain below. Students then write the words.

| rain | raid | read | real | steal |
|---|---|---|---|---|

## Make It Harder

Students who can manipulate phonemes in grade-level words may be ready to work in pairs to manipulate sounds and create their own word chain.

- Create a set of word cards with each of these words: *steam, boast, groom, glow.*
- Place the word cards in a pile with the words facing down. The first student flips over a card. Students work in pairs to create a word chain, starting with the first word. They write the words from their word chain and identify which sound has changed in each word.
- The second student flips over the next card and they create another word chain, starting with the new word. Continue with the remaining word cards.
- Students then create sentences with some of the words from their word chain.

SIDE A

# Reverse Phonemes

**Phoneme reversal,** a part of **phoneme manipulation,** is the ability to say the sounds of a word backward to create a new word.

## ROUTINE

### STEP 1 INTRODUCE

We can reverse, or say the sounds of a word backward, to create a new word. Today we will practice reversing the sounds of a word to make a new word.

### STEP 2 MODEL

- Slide your hand down your arm as you say the sounds of the word. Listen to this word: *charm* /ch/ (touch your shoulder) /är/ (slide to your elbow) /m/ (slide down to your hand).
- Move your hand up your arm. (Remember to reverse the *sounds* rather than the *letters.*) This time, I will say the sounds in reverse: /m/ (touch your hand) /är/ (slide to your elbow) /ch/ (slide up to your shoulder). The new word is *march.*
- **Phonics Connection** Write *charm* and *march.* Discuss how the order of the sound-spellings has changed. When I look at *charm* and *march,* I notice that the /ch/ and /m/ have changed places.

### STEP 3 GUIDE PRACTICE

- Slide your hand down your arm as you sound out the word. *Serve:* /s/ /ėr/ /v/. Now say the sounds backward, starting from your hand and moving up: /v/ /ėr/ /s/. What's the new word? (*verse*)
- **Phonics Connection** Write *serve* and *verse.* What do you notice about the sound-spellings in these words? Discuss the differences with students.

### STEP 4 ON THEIR OWN

Have students repeat this routine with the words below.

| | | | |
|---|---|---|---|
| seal/lease | back/cab | loaf/foal | sake/case |
| tick/kit | dill/lid | ooze/zoo | mood/doom |

**SIDE B**

# Reverse Phonemes

**CORRECTIVE FEEDBACK**

| | |
|---|---|
| **IF** students cannot reverse phonemes, | **THEN** work through the Make It Easier activity and review Steps 2 and 3 if needed. |

## Make It Easier

Students who cannot reverse phonemes in grade-level words may use counters to practice in tapping and manipulating phonemes.

- Listen to this word: *eat.* How many sounds do you hear? (*two*) Take out two counters and tap the sounds of the word. (/ē/ /t/, *eat*)
- Now tap the second counter, then the first counter, and say the sounds backward. What are the sounds? (/t/ /ē/, *tea*)
- Continue with the words below.

| | | |
|---|---|---|
| **deaf/fed** | **loop/pool** | **cat/tack** |
| **tale/late** | **face/safe** | **neat/teen** |

## Make It Harder

Students who can reverse phonemes may work in pairs to identify the different sound-spelling patterns in words with similar sounds.

- Create a set of word cards with the words below.

| | | | |
|---|---|---|---|
| **might/time** | **zone/nose** | **sign/nice** | **peel/leap** |
| **pitch/chip** | **seen/niece** | **badge/jab** | |

- The first student will choose a word card and read the word. The second student will work to say the sounds of the word backward to identify the new word.
- Both students work together to discuss how the sound-spelling patterns are different in the two words. They then write sentences with the words.
- The second student then chooses a card and reads it to the first student. The first student repeats the steps above.

# Word Study

- High-Frequency Words Routines
- Syllable Patterns Routines

See SavvasRealize.com for additional practice activities.

SIDE A

# Syllable Pattern VC/CV

WORD STUDY
GRADE 3

A **syllable** is a word part that has one vowel sound. Words with the VC/CV syllable pattern have two syllables.

**Connect to *myView Literacy:***
**Syllable Pattern:**
Unit 1, p. T22

**See digital practice on SavvasRealize.com.**

## ROUTINE

### STEP 1 INTRODUCE

Breaking words into syllables can help you read longer words. Today we will practice reading words with the vowel-consonant-consonant-vowel, or VC/CV, syllable pattern.

### STEP 2 MODEL

- Display the word *ladder*. The word *ladder* has the syllable pattern VC/CV. Point to the letters *adde* as you identify them. Words with the VC/CV pattern have two consonants in the middle. We divide the word into syllables between the two consonants, *d* and *d*. Now I see the two syllables, *lad* and *der*. I can blend the syllables and read the word: lad/der, *ladder*.

**ladder**

**lad / der**

- Display the word *sister*. I'll find the pattern in this word. Point to the letters *iste* and say: vowel, consonant, consonant, vowel.

**sister**

- Now that I've found the VC/CV pattern, I will divide the word into syllables. I'll divide between the two consonants, *s* and *t*. Point to each syllable as you say: sis/ter. Now I'll blend: sis/ter, *sister*.

**sis / ter**

### STEP 3 GUIDE PRACTICE

Display the word *corner*. What letters spell the VC/CV pattern? (*orne*) Where do we divide this word into syllables? (between the two consonants, *r* and *n*) What are the two syllables? (cor/ner) Let's read the word: cor/ner, *corner*.

**corner**

**cor / ner**

### STEP 4 ON THEIR OWN

Have students identify the VC/CV pattern in each word, divide the word into syllables, and then blend the syllables to read the word.

| hammer | permit | upper | center |
|---|---|---|---|
| ham / mer | per / mit | up / per | cen / ter |

**SIDE B**

# Syllable Pattern VC/CV

**WORD STUDY**
**GRADE 3**

## CORRECTIVE FEEDBACK

**IF** students cannot divide a word with the VC/CV pattern into syllables,

**THEN** model identifying the pattern and dividing words, using Steps 2 and 3. Next, work through the Make It Easier activity.

## Make It Easier

Some students may benefit from revisiting one-syllable CVC words.

- Display the word *sun*. This word has one syllable. What is the vowel in the middle? (*u*) Point to each letter and say: consonant, vowel, consonant. Write *CVC* above *sun*. A CVC word almost always has a short vowel sound. Listen: *sun*. Say it with me: *sun*.
- Continue as above. Display each CVC word at the right. Guide students to identify the CVC pattern and then read the word.
- Now let's look at a two-syllable word. Display *sunset*. Reading a word one syllable at a time helps us know how to say each part. Underline *unse* as you say: This word has a vowel, consonant, consonant, vowel pattern. We divide words with this pattern between the two consonants: *sun/set*. Sweep your hand under each syllable as you say: *sun/set, sunset.*
- Repeat the step above with the word *kitten*.
- Display *sunlit* and *mitten*. Guide students, as needed, to identify the VC/CV pattern, divide each word, and read it.

**sun**

**set** **kit** **ten**

**sunset**

**sun / set**

| | |
|---|---|
| **kitten** | **kit / ten** |
| **sunlit** | **sun / lit** |
| **mitten** | **mit / ten** |

## Make It Harder

Students who can divide words with the VC/CV pattern into syllables may enjoy an extension activity.

- Have students list VC/CV words that they find in classroom texts. Partners then exchange lists and divide the words into syllables.
- Then have partners check each other's divisions and read aloud the words.

SIDE A

# Inflected Endings -*s*, -*es*, -*ies*

**WORD STUDY**
GRADE 3

An **inflected ending** is a letter or group of letters added to a base word that changes the word's tense, voice, or number.

**Connect to *myView Literacy:***
**Inflected Endings:** Unit 1, p. T92

**See digital practice on SavvasRealize.com.**

## ROUTINE

### STEP 1 INTRODUCE

To make a singular noun plural, add an ending. Display cards showing the endings -*s*, -*es*, and -*ies*. Point to each ending as you say: Add an -*s* ending to most nouns to make them plural. For other nouns, add the ending -*es* or -*ies*.

**s** **es** **ies**

### STEP 2 MODEL

- Display the word *task*. Slide the -*s* card next to *task* as you say: The singular form is *task;* one task. We add -*s* to make the plural form: two tasks. This is how we form most plural nouns.

**task / tasks**

- Display the word *bench*. Slide the -*es* card next to *bench*. For *bench*, I add -*es* to form the plural: two benches. We add -*es* when a singular noun ends in *sh, ch, tch, s, ss,* or *x*. *Bench* ends in *ch*, so I added -*es* to make it plural.

**bench / benches**

- Display the word *story*. The singular noun *story* ends in a consonant + *y*. In nouns that end in a consonant + *y*, we change the *y* to *i* and then add -*es*. Position the -*ies* card so it covers the *y* of *story*. Now I have the plural: two stories.

**story / stories**

### STEP 3 GUIDE PRACTICE

Display and point to each noun. *Tube* is like most nouns. What ending do we add to make *tube* plural? (-*s*) *Marsh* ends in *sh*. What ending do we add to make *marsh* plural? (-*es*) *Body* ends in a consonant + *y*. What ending will make *body* plural? (-*ies*)

**tube**
**marsh**
**body**

### STEP 4 ON THEIR OWN

Have students form the plurals of these nouns.

**speck** **fox** **county** **slope** **baby** **mess**

**SIDE B**

# Inflected Endings *-s, -es, -ies*

### CORRECTIVE FEEDBACK

| | |
|---|---|
| **IF** students cannot form plural nouns by adding the ending *-s, -es,* or *-ies,* | **THEN** model how to form plural nouns, using Steps 2 and 3. Next, work through the Make It Easier activity. |

## Make It Easier

Students who struggle to form plural nouns correctly may benefit from a tactile approach using cards or tiles.

- Distribute cards for the ending *-s* and the words at the right. *Hill* is singular. How do we make it plural? (by adding *-s*) Have students slide the *s* in place at the end of the word. What is the plural form of *hill?* (*hills*) Repeat with the other words. (*cakes, windows*)
- Display cards for the ending *-es* and the words at the right. *Flash* is a singular noun. Listen to the ending sound: /sh/. How do we make *flash* plural? (by adding *-es*) Have students slide the *es* card in place. What is the plural form of *flash?* (*flashes*) Repeat with the other words. (*dresses, porches, patches, boxes, buses*)
- Display cards for the ending *-ies* and the words at the right. *Daisy* is a singular noun. How do we make *daisy* plural? (by changing the *y* to *i* and adding *es*) Have students slide the *ies* card over the *y*. What is the plural form of *daisy?* (*daisies*) Repeat with the other words. (*puppies, pennies*)

s

hill
cake
window

es

flash
porch
box
dress
patch
bus

ies

daisy
puppy
penny

## Make It Harder

Students who can form plural nouns correctly can play a game with a partner. Provide paper and pencil, dry-erase boards, or tablets.

- The first student writes a word and says, for example: *I have one bunny. Please give me two.* The partner responds by writing the plural form: *bunnies.*
- Both partners approve of the plural word form. Then students switch roles and continue.
- Provide words for students: *hand, bicycle, library, ash, pony, bush, latch, arch, ostrich.*

WORD STUDY
GRADE 3

**SIDE A**

# Base Words and Endings *-ing, -ed, -er, -est*

Connect to *myView Literacy:*
**Base Words and Endings:**
Unit 1, p. T154

A **base word** is the simplest form of a word. It can stand alone, or endings or affixes may be added.

## ROUTINE

**See digital practice on SavvasRealize.com.**

### STEP 1 INTRODUCE

Adding an ending to a base word changes the base word's meaning. Display the endings. We can add *-ing* and *-ed* to verbs to tell when the action happens. Add *-er* and *-est* to most short adjectives to compare.

| | |
|---|---|
| ing | ed |
| er | est |

### STEP 2 MODEL

- Display the verb *glow*. Slide each ending in place as you say: I add *-ing* to the end of a verb to tell what is happening now; *glowing.* I add *-ed* to a verb to tell what happened in the past; *glowed*. Repeat with *shop,* but add: For some base words, we double the final consonant and then add the ending.
- Display *nice, nicer, nicest*. An adjective with the *-er* ending compares two people or things. An adjective with *-est* compares three or more. For words that end in silent *e,* we drop the *e* before adding the ending. Repeat with *shiny,* but add: For words that end in a consonant + *y,* we change the *y* to *i* before adding the ending.

glow ing

glow ed

shop
shopping
shopped

### STEP 3 GUIDE PRACTICE

- Display *smile.* What ending do we add to the verb to show action happening now? (*-ing*) To show action happened in the past? (*-ed*)
- Display *fast.* What ending do we add to compare two things? (*-er*) To compare three or more? (*-est*)

### STEP 4 ON THEIR OWN

For the words at the right, have students add *-ing* and *-ed* to the verbs and *-er* and *-est* to the adjectives. Then have them spell the new word and use it in a sentence.

| | |
|---|---|
| scrape | dash |
| stir | green |
| creamy | pale |

SIDE B

# Base Words and Endings *-ing, -ed, -er, -est*

### CORRECTIVE FEEDBACK

**IF** students cannot tell how an ending changes the meaning of a base word,

**THEN** model adding endings to change meaning, using Steps 2 and 3. Next, work through the Make It Easier activity.

## Make It Easier

Students may benefit from examining words in context.

- Display the verb *bake* and the sentences. Read each sentence aloud and underline clues that reveal when the action happens. What ending is added to *bake* to show that action is happening now? (*-ing*) What ending shows that action happened yesterday? (*-ed*)
- Display the adjective *flat* and the sentences. Read each sentence aloud and underline clues that indicate the number of things being compared. What ending is added to *flat* to compare two things? (*-er*) What ending shows three or more things are compared? (*-est*)
- Display the sentences below. Have students complete each sentence with the correct form of the word in parentheses.

  At the cookout last night, we ____ lots of marshmallows. (roast)
  Angel hair pasta is ____ than regular spaghetti. (thin)

**bake**

We bake every week.

We are baking bread today.

We baked a cake yesterday.

**flat**

My front tire is flat.

The back tire is flatter than the front tire.

Your bike tire is the flattest of all.

## Make It Harder

Offer this extension activity for students who can tell how endings change word meanings.

- Provide the following verbs and adjectives: *cleaning, listened, tried, closer, bumpiest, hotter.*
- Have students write sentences using each word correctly. Then have partners share sentences and peer edit, as needed, to correct usage and spelling.

**SIDE A**

# Vowel Digraphs *ee, ea, ai, ay, ow, oa*

**Connect to *myView Literacy:***
**Vowel Digraphs:** Unit 1, p. T216

**Vowel digraphs** are letter combinations that spell one vowel sound.

**See digital practice on SavvasRealize.com.**

## ROUTINE

### STEP 1 INTRODUCE

A vowel digraph is two letters that spell one vowel sound. The vowel sound is usually the long vowel sound of the first vowel. Knowing the sounds for digraphs can help you read words.

ee ea ai
ay ow oa

### STEP 2 MODEL

- Display the word *meet.* Underline the vowel digraph. I see the vowel digraph *ee.* The vowel digraph *ee* can spell the sound /ē/. This is how I blend the sounds in the word *meet.* Point to each sound spelling as you say its sound: /m/ /ē/ /t/, *meet.*
- Repeat for the remaining digraphs using the words *heat, brain, clay, row,* and *toad.*

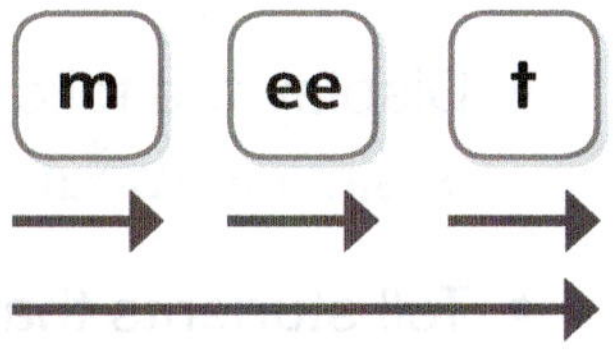


### STEP 3 GUIDE PRACTICE

- Display the word *beat*. Let's try this word. Which vowel digraph do you see? (*ea*) What sound can the vowel digraph *ea* make? (/ē/) Sweep your hand under *beat* as students blend the sounds to read the word with you: /b/ /ē/ /t/, *beat.*
- Repeat for these words: *feel, sail, tray, crow,* and *soak.*

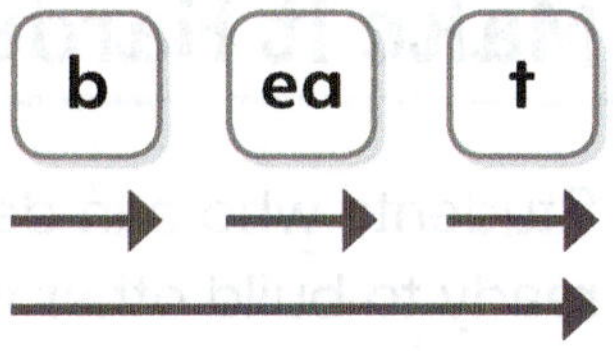


### STEP 4 ON THEIR OWN

Display word cards for the following words: *feet, leaf, train, days, blow,* and *coach.* Have students identify the vowel digraph and the vowel sound it can spell for each word. Then have students read aloud each word.

SIDE B

# Vowel Digraphs *ee, ea, ai, ay, ow, oa*

**CORRECTIVE FEEDBACK**

**IF** students cannot decode words with vowel digraphs *ee, ea, ai, ay, ow*, or *oa,*

**THEN** model how to decode words with these digraphs, using Steps 2 and 3. Next, work through the Make It Easier activity.

## Make It Easier

Students who cannot decode words with vowel digraphs that spell a long vowel sound may benefit from more practice with long vowel spellings.

- Display the following words: *go, note, show,* and *goat.* Read aloud the words. Ask: What is similar about all of these words? Right. Each word has the long *o* sound.
- Tell students that the long *o* sound can be spelled in different ways. Have students underline the long *o* spelling in each word.
- Repeat with the following words and the long *a* sound: *date, rain,* and *pay*. Then repeat for these words and the long *e* sound: *need, read, me,* and *Pete.*

## Make It Harder

Students who can decode words with vowel digraphs that spell a long vowel sound may be ready to build other words.

- Have students use letter tiles or cards to build a word with a long vowel sound for each of the following vowel digraphs: *ee, ea, ai, ay, ow, oa*.
- Have partners challenge each other to read aloud the words they built and to use each word in a sentence.

WORD STUDY
GRADE 3

**SIDE A**

# Diphthongs *ou, ow, oi, oy*

A **diphthong** is a single vowel sound, represented by two letters, that resembles a glide from one sound to another.

**Connect to *myView Literacy:***
**Diphthongs:** Unit 1, p. T286

## ROUTINE

**See digital practice on SavvasRealize.com.**

### STEP 1 INTRODUCE

A diphthong is two letters that spell one vowel sound. Knowing the different spellings for the same vowel sound can help you read and spell more words.

| | |
|---|---|
| ou | ow |
| oi | oy |

### STEP 2 MODEL

- Display the words *mouse* and *down.* Underline *ou* and *ow*. Different combinations of letters can spell the same vowel sound. The letters *ou* and *ow* in these words both spell the same vowel sound: /ou/. Read aloud each word: *mouse, down.*
- Display the words *boil* and *boy.* Underline *oi* and *oy*. The letters *oi* and *oy* in these words both spell the same vowel sound: /oi/. Read aloud each word: *boil, boy.*

| | |
|---|---|
| mouse | down |
| boil | boy |

### STEP 3 GUIDE PRACTICE

- Display the word *plow*. Let's try this word. Have students underline the letters that spell the diphthong and then read aloud the word.
- Repeat for the words *house, join,* and *joy.*

| | |
|---|---|
| plow | join |
| house | joy |

### STEP 4 ON THEIR OWN

In pairs, have students take turns reading and then writing the words at the right. Have them underline the letters that spell the diphthong in each word.

| | |
|---|---|
| pout | coin |
| cow | toys |

SIDE B

# Diphthongs *ou, ow, oi, oy*

**CORRECTIVE FEEDBACK**

**IF** students cannot decode a word with a diphthong,

**THEN** model how to blend each sound spelling in the word, using Steps 2 and 3. Next, work through the Make It Easier activity.

## Make It Easier

Students who have difficulty reading words with diphthongs may benefit from practice with one sound spelling at a time.

- Display the word *out*. Underline the *ou* as you say: The letters *o* and *u* work together to spell one sound, /ou/. Say it with me: /ou/. Have students blend the sounds to say the word with you.
- Display the words *mouse* and *shout.* Ask students to underline the letters that spell the diphthong in each word and identify its sound. Then have them blend the sounds to read aloud the word.
- Repeat for the letters that spell the diphthongs in the words *now, coil,* and *coy.*

**out**
**mouse**
**shout**

**now**
**coil**
**coy**

## Make It Harder

Students who can read words with diphthongs may be ready to write words.

- Have students write a list of words for each spelling *ou, ow, oi,* and *oy* for diphthongs /ou/ and /oi/. Challenge them to write two-syllable words with each of the diphthongs, such as *appoint* and *flower.*
- Then have them choose one word from each list and write a sentence using the word.

SIDE A

# Syllable Patterns VC/V and V/CV

A **syllable** is a word part that has one vowel sound. Words with the syllable pattern VCV can be divided before or after the consonant.

Connect to *myView Literacy:*
**Syllable Patterns:** Unit 2, p. T22

See digital practice on SavvasRealize.com.

## ROUTINE

### STEP 1 INTRODUCE

Review with students that words have different syllable patterns. Knowing where to divide words into syllables can help you read longer words. Today we will practice reading words with the syllable pattern VCV.

### STEP 2 MODEL

- Display the word *spider* and point out the VCV pattern. When there is one consonant between two vowels, we usually divide before the consonant. Divide the word into syllables before the consonant *d*. Read aloud each syllable and then blend: spi/der, *spider*. Point out that when the first syllable ends in a vowel, the vowel sound is long.
- Display the word *habit*. Now I'll try it with this word. I'll divide before the consonant. Hā/bit, *hābit*. I'm not familiar with *hābit*, so I'll divide after the consonant. I'm familiar with *habit*. This word is *habit*. Point out that when the first syllable ends in a consonant, the vowel sound is short.

| |
|---|
| spider |
| spi / der |
| habit |
| hab / it |

### STEP 3 GUIDE PRACTICE

- Display the word *pilot*. Is there one consonant between two vowels? (yes) Where do we usually divide? (before the consonant) Divide the word. Say each syllable and then say the word. (pi/lot, *pilot*) Is *pilot* a familiar word? (yes)
- Repeat with the word *robin*, first dividing before the consonant and then dividing after the consonant to read the word correctly.

| |
|---|
| pilot |
| pi / lot |
| robin |
| rob / in |

### STEP 4 ON THEIR OWN

Have partners divide each word at the right into syllables—first by dividing before the consonant, and if that is not a familiar word, by dividing after the consonant. Then have them read the word and discuss its meaning.

| | |
|---|---|
| visit | donut |
| music | comet |

SIDE B

# Syllable Patterns VC/V and V/CV

**CORRECTIVE FEEDBACK**

**IF** students have difficulty dividing and reading words with the VCV pattern,

**THEN** model reading words with the VCV pattern again, using Steps 2 and 3. Next, work through the Make It Easier activity.

## Make It Easier

Students may benefit from practicing only with words that have the V/CV pattern.

- Review that most words with the VCV pattern are divided before the consonant, and that when a syllable ends in a vowel, the vowel sound is long.
- Display the word *tulip.* Point to the letter *u.* Is this letter a vowel or consonant? (vowel) Write a *V* above the *u.* Repeat for the letters *l* and *i,* writing *C* above *l* and *V* above *i.*
- What is the vowel pattern? (VCV) Do I divide before or after the consonant? (before) Divide the word. The first syllable ends in a vowel. Is the vowel sound long or short? (long) Have students read each syllable and then the word.
- Then have students divide and read these words.

**tulip**

**tu / lip**

**open** **robot** **pupil** **hotel**

## Make It Harder

Provide an extension activity for students who can divide words with the VCV pattern.

- Tell students that words can have more than one pattern. Display three-syllable words with the VCV pattern and the VCCV pattern. Review the VCCV pattern as needed.
- Have partners work together to divide and read each word at the right. Guide students to identify the syllable pattern in the first two syllables before moving on to identify the pattern in the third syllable.

**potato**

**acrobat**

**volcano**

**coconut**

**SIDE A**

**WORD STUDY**
GRADE 3

# *r*-Controlled Vowels *ar, or, ore, oar*

An ***r*-controlled vowel** refers to a vowel or vowel pattern followed by the letter *r* that has neither a long vowel sound nor a short vowel sound, but an *r*-controlled vowel sound.

**Connect to *myView Literacy:***
***r*-Controlled Vowels:** Unit 2, p. T84

**See digital practice on SavvasRealize.com.**

# ROUTINE

## STEP 1 INTRODUCE

An *r*-controlled vowel is a vowel or vowel pattern followed by the letter *r*. The *r* changes the sound of the vowel or vowel pattern to a sound that is neither long nor short. Today we'll learn to read words that have the *r*-controlled vowel sound /är/ you hear in *jar* and the sound /ôr/ you hear in *more.*

| | |
|---|---|
| **ar** | **or** |
| **ore** | **oar** |

## STEP 2 MODEL

- Display and read aloud the word *party*. I hear the sound /är/ in the middle of *party.* Underline *ar*. The letters *ar* spell the sound /är/ in *party.* Blend the sounds to read *party*.
- Display and read aloud the words *organ, forehead,* and *blackboard*. I hear the sound /ôr/ in each of these words. Underline *or, ore,* and *oar.* The letters *or, ore,* and *oar* all spell the sound /ôr/. Blend the sounds to read the words.

**party**

**organ**

**forehead**

**blackboard**

## STEP 3 GUIDE PRACTICE

- Display the word *hornet*. Which *r*-controlled vowel pattern do you see? (*or*) What sound does the vowel pattern spell? (/ôr/) Sweep your hand under *hornet* as students blend the sounds to read the word with you.
- Repeat for these words: *farmhouse, shoreline,* and *clipboard.*

**hornet**

**farmhouse**

**shoreline**

**clipboard**

## STEP 4 ON THEIR OWN

Have students read aloud the following words and identify the *r*-controlled vowel pattern: *barnyard, shorten, scorecard,* and *roaring.* Then have them use the words in sentences.

SIDE B

# *r*-Controlled Vowels *ar, or, ore, oar*

### CORRECTIVE FEEDBACK

| | |
|---|---|
| **IF** students cannot decode words with an *r*-controlled vowel or vowel pattern, | **THEN** model how to blend each sound-spelling in words, using Steps 2 and 3. Next, work through the Make It Easier activity. |

## Make It Easier

Students who cannot blend the sounds in multisyllabic words with *r*-controlled vowels may benefit from practice with one-syllable words.

- Display the word *car.* Underline the *ar* as you say: The *r*-controlled vowel sound /är/ in *car* can be spelled *ar.* Have students blend the sounds to say the word with you.
- Have students underline the *r*-controlled vowel pattern in the following words: *smart, harm,* and *sharp.* Then have them blend the sounds to read the words.
- Continue by focusing on the other *r*-controlled spellings one at a time. Use the following words for the sound /ôr/ spelled *or, ore,* and *oar*: *for, cord, fort; more, shore, core; soar, coarse, oar.*

## Make It Harder

Students who can read words with *r*-controlled vowels spelled *ar, or, ore*, and *oar* may be ready to write words with these *r*-controlled vowel patterns.

- Have students create lists of words for each of the *r*-controlled vowel patterns *ar, or, ore,* and *oar*.
- Next, have students read aloud the words their partner listed.
- Finally, have partners write sentences using words with each of the *r*-controlled vowel patterns.

SIDE A

# Compound Words

**Compound words** are made of two or more smaller words.

**Connect to *myView Literacy:***
**Compound Words:** Unit 2, p. T146

See digital practice on SavvasRealize.com.

# ROUTINE

## STEP 1 INTRODUCE

Identifying the smaller words that make up a compound word can help you read the compound word and figure out its meaning.

## STEP 2 MODEL

- Display the word *sunrise*. I see a word that has two smaller, familiar words in it. Underline each word part as you say: The two words are *sun* and *rise*. When they are combined, they make a new, compound word: *sunrise*.
- When I see a compound word, I can sometimes use the meanings of the two smaller words to figure out the meaning of the compound word. *Sunrise* means "the time when the sun rises."
- Let's look at another compound word. Underline each word part as you say: I see the smaller words *race* and *track* in this longer word. The compound word is *racetrack*. If I put the two words' meanings together, I can figure out that a *racetrack* means "a track for racing."

**sunrise**

**racetrack**

## STEP 3 GUIDE PRACTICE

Display the word *newspaper*. What smaller words do you see in this word? (*news* and *paper*) What is the compound word? (*newspaper*) What does *newspaper* mean? ("a paper that contains news") Repeat with *rowboat*. (*row* and *boat;* "a boat that is rowed")

**newspaper**

**rowboat**

## STEP 4 ON THEIR OWN

Have students identify the smaller words that make up each compound word and then tell the meaning of the compound word.

**starfish** **doorbell** **horseshoe** **spaceship**

SIDE B

# Compound Words

### CORRECTIVE FEEDBACK

**IF** students cannot decode compound words and determine meaning,

**THEN** model identifying the smaller words in compound words to determine meaning, using Steps 2 and 3. Next, work through the Make It Easier activity.

## Make It Easier

Students may benefit from a tactile approach.

- Prepare cards with these words: *snow, flake, man, day, dream, light.*
- Display the *snow* and *flake* cards, but not close together. We can form a compound word from these two smaller words. Read them with me: *snow, flake.*
- Direct students to slide the two cards together. You have made a new word. Let's read it together: *snowflake.* Have students slide the cards apart, read the words separately, and slide them together again.
- Repeat in a similar manner with the remaining cards to form these words: *snowman, daydream, daylight*.
- Prepare word cards with the words at the right. Have students read each word. Then have them position the cards to form compound words and read the compound words. (*sunburn, sunset, sunglasses*)

| snow | flake |
|---|---|

| snowflake |
|---|

| | |
|---|---|
| sun | burn |
| set | glasses |

## Make It Harder

Students who can decode and determine the meaning of compound words can "hide" the parts of compound words in sentences and challenge a partner to find them.

- Provide students with several compound words, or have students choose their own words.
- Have individual students write a sentence using the two words of each compound word. For example, a sentence for *cowbell* might be: *I think that cow has a bell.*
- Partners exchange sentences, locate the words, and form the compound word.

**WORD STUDY**
GRADE 3

**SIDE A**

# Syllable Pattern VC*e*

A **syllable** is a word part that has one vowel sound. Syllables with the pattern VC*e* have a long vowel sound.

**Connect to *myView Literacy:***
**Syllable Patterns:** Unit 2, p. T206

**See digital practice on SavvasRealize.com.**

## ROUTINE

### STEP 1 INTRODUCE

Review with students that words have different syllable patterns. Recognizing the syllable pattern VC*e* can help you read longer words. Today we will practice reading words with the final syllable pattern VC*e*.

### STEP 2 MODEL

- Display the word *hid.* Have students read aloud the word. The vowel *i* in *hid* spells the short *i* sound /i/.

**hid**

- Add *e* to the end of *hid* and point to *e*. The *e* at the end of a vowel-consonant-*e*, or VC*e*, word usually changes the first vowel to a long sound. The *e* is silent. Underline *ide*. The letters *ide* spell the VC*e* pattern, so the first vowel, *i*, is long and the *e* is silent. This word is *hide*.

**hide**

- Display the word *bedtime.* I can use what I know about the VC*e* pattern to help me read longer words. I will look at the last three letters of this word. Point to *ime*: I see the vowel *i*, the consonant *m*, and the vowel *e* at the end of the word. This is the VC*e* pattern, so I know that the vowel *i* is long and the *e* is silent. The final syllable is *time.* The word is *bedtime.*

**bedtime**

### STEP 3 GUIDE PRACTICE

- Display *tadpole.* Have students look for a VC*e* pattern. What letters spell a VC*e* pattern in this word? (*ole*) What is the final syllable? (*pole*) What is the word? (*tadpole*)

**tadpole**

- Repeat with the word *escape.*

**escape**

### STEP 4 ON THEIR OWN

Display the following words: *costume, flagpole, mistake, reptile.* Have students identify the VC*e* pattern in each word and then read the words.

**SIDE B**

# Syllable Pattern VC*e*

**WORD STUDY**
**GRADE 3**

## CORRECTIVE FEEDBACK

**IF** students have difficulty reading longer words with the VC*e* pattern,

**THEN** model reading words with the VC*e* pattern again, using Steps 2 and 3. Next, work through the Make It Easier activity.

## Make It Easier

Students who cannot read longer words with the VC*e* pattern may benefit from reading and sorting one-syllable words with the VC*e* pattern.

- Say: Remember that in words with the VC*e* pattern, the first vowel is long and the final *e* is silent.
- Provide partners with a set of these word cards. Have them sort the cards into groups based on the vowel sound.
- Then have them take turns reading each word. Have students explain why the vowel sound is long.

| | |
|---|---|
| white | broke |
| made | theme |
| throne | cube |
| slide | plane |
| prune | flame |

## Make It Harder

Students who can read longer words with the VC*e* pattern may enjoy combining syllables to make new words with the VC*e* pattern.

- Create cards with these syllables. Mix up the cards and provide a set to partners.
- Have partners work together to write as many words as they can by combining syllables. Then have them use each new word in a sentence.

| | |
|---|---|
| bag | pipe |
| ship | mate |
| cup | cake |
| in | side |
| lunch | time |
| sun | rise |

**SIDE A**

# Contractions

**WORD STUDY**
GRADE 3

A **contraction** is a shortened form of two words. Some letters of one word are removed and replaced with an apostrophe.

**Connect to *myView Literacy:***
**Contractions:** Unit 2, p. T268

**See digital practice on SavvasRealize.com.**

## ROUTINE

### STEP 1 INTRODUCE

Some of the words we often use are contractions. Recognizing a contraction and identifying the two original words will help you read the contraction and figure out its meaning.

### STEP 2 MODEL

- Display the word *I've*. One clue that *I've* is a contraction is the apostrophe. Contractions are made up of two words. Underline each word part as you say: The first word is *I*. The second word is *have,* but the contraction includes only the last two letters. The apostrophe takes the place of the letters *ha*.
- Display *do* and *not*. Now I'll form a contraction. I know that when *not* is part of a contraction, the *o* is removed; that's where the apostrophe goes. Display or manipulate cards to show *don't.* A contraction doesn't always sound like the original words. Notice how the *o* sound is different in *do* and *don't.*

**I've**

**I have**

**do not**

**don't**

### STEP 3 GUIDE PRACTICE

Display the word *we'll*. What two words were combined to form the contraction? (*we, will*) What letters were removed? (*wi* from *will*) What takes the place of the letters? (an apostrophe) Read the contraction with me: *we'll.*

**we'll**

### STEP 4 ON THEIR OWN

Have students read each word and tell what two words form the contraction.

| | | | |
|---|---|---|---|
| let's | she's | they're | would've |

# Contractions



### CORRECTIVE FEEDBACK

**IF** students cannot read contractions and identify the words used to form them,

**THEN** model the process, using Steps 2 and 3. Next, work through the Make It Easier activity.

## Make It Easier

Students might benefit from practice with common types of contractions.

- Let's focus on contractions with *not.* One contraction formed with *not* is *doesn't.* It is made up of the words *does* + *not.* The apostrophe replaces the *o* in *not.* Display the words at the right. For each word, ask, Which words form the contraction? Which letter(s) does the apostrophe replace?
- Next focus on contractions with *have.* One contraction formed with *have* is *you've,* from the words *you* + *have.* The apostrophe replaces the *ha* in *have.* Display the words at the right. For each word, ask, Which words make up the contraction? Which letter(s) does the apostrophe replace?
- Continue with contractions formed with *is,* such as *it's* and *that's.*

**didn't**

**wouldn't**

**shouldn't**

**we've**

**they've**

## Make It Harder

Students who can read contractions and identify the words that form them may enjoy an extension activity.

- Tell students that they are to become Contraction Detectives.
- First, have partners look around the room and list contractions they see on posters, bulletin boards, student work, and so on. Then have the partners look in a text they are reading and list contractions they find there.
- Have the partners identify the words that make up each contraction. Then have them sort their lists into categories. For example, Contractions with *not,* Contractions with *will,* and so on. Have students find patterns in how contractions are formed within each category.

**WORD STUDY**
**GRADE 3**

**SIDE A**

# Prefixes *pre-, dis-, in-, im-, non-*

A **prefix** is a group of letters added to the beginning of a word that changes the meaning of the word.

**Connect to *myView Literacy:***
**Prefixes *pre-, dis-, in-, im-, non-*:**
Unit 3, p. T22

**See digital practice on SavvasRealize.com.**

## ROUTINE

### STEP 1 INTRODUCE

Display cards with the prefixes *pre-, dis-, in-, im-,* and *non-*. When we add a prefix to a base word, we create a new word with a new meaning. Knowing the meaning of the prefix is a strategy you can use to help figure out the meaning of a longer word.

**pre** **dis** **in**
**im** **non**

### STEP 2 MODEL

- Display the word *cook*. Position the *pre* card in front of *cook* as you say: I know what *cook* means, but what about *precook?* I know that the prefix *pre-* means "before." So I can figure out that *precook* means "to cook before."
- The prefixes *dis-, in-, im-,* and *non-* all mean "not." Display the word *allow*. Position the *dis* card in front of *allow* as you say: I know what *allow* means. When I know that the prefix *dis-* means "not," I can figure out that *disallow* means "not allow."
- Repeat in a similar manner with *insecure, impure,* and *nonglossy*.

**pre** **cook**

**dis** **allow**

### STEP 3 GUIDE PRACTICE

Display the word *mix*. What prefix can we add to make a word that means "to mix before"? (*pre-*) Display the word *skid*. If I add the prefix *non-* to this word, what does the new word mean? (does not skid)

**mix**

**skid**

### STEP 4 ON THEIR OWN

Have students identify the base word and the prefix in the words below. Then have them tell what the word means.

**disloyal** **inactive** **nonwoven** **preowned** **imbalance**

**SIDE B**

# Prefixes *pre-, dis-, in-, im-, non-*

## CORRECTIVE FEEDBACK

**IF** students cannot tell how the prefixes change the meaning of a base word,

**THEN** model how each prefix changes a word's meaning, using Steps 2 and 3. Next, work through the Make It Easier activity.

## Make It Easier

Students who struggle with prefixes may benefit from determining the meaning of words in context.

- Display and read aloud the two sentences. Which sentence makes more sense? (the second one) Why? (because a person might frown and throw away a ticket that is "not a winner") Which word means "not a winner"? (*nonwinning*)
- Display and read aloud the two sentences. Which sentence makes more sense? (the first one) Why? (because pilots would put suits on "before" the launch) Which word means "before the launch"? (*prelaunch*)
- Continue the activity with additional sentence pairs showing words with and without prefixes.

Ari frowned and threw away his winning ticket.

Ari frowned and threw away his nonwinning ticket.

During the prelaunch process, the pilots put on flight suits.

During the launch process, the pilots put on flight suits.

## Make It Harder

Students can play a matching game to build new words and determine their meanings.

- Provide cards with prefixes and words as shown at the right. Have partners lay the cards face down in two rows—prefixes and base words.
- The first student chooses a card from each row and tells whether the two cards form a word. If so, the student says the word and its meaning. If not, the student returns the cards and the partner takes a turn. Play continues until partners have formed five words.

**pre- dis- in-**
**im- non-**

**sensitive paid**
**mobile sense**
**respect**

**SIDE A**

# Abbreviations

**Abbreviations** are shortened forms of longer words or phrases. Abbreviations use some letters from the original word or words.

**Connect to *myView Literacy:***
**Abbreviations:** Unit 3, p. T92

See digital practice on SavvasRealize.com.

## ROUTINE

### STEP 1 INTRODUCE

You can recognize abbreviations because most of them begin with a capital letter and end with a period. When you read an abbreviation, you say the word as if it were spelled out.

### STEP 2 MODEL

- Display the two phrases at the right. Sometimes when we write, we abbreviate a word, or make it shorter. Here is the name of a road. The first version is written out completely. The second version shows an abbreviation for the word *Road.*
- Point as you say: The abbreviation uses the first and last letter of the original word: *R* and *d.* The abbreviation has a capital letter, just like the original word. But the abbreviation adds a period at the end. I read both of these phrases the same way: *Robin Road.*

**Robin Road**

**Robin Rd.**

### STEP 3 GUIDE PRACTICE

Display the noun *Mt. Shasta.* What word is abbreviated? (*Mount* is abbreviated as *Mt.*) How do you know? (It has a capital letter and a period.) How do we read the abbreviation? (We say *mount,* just as if it were spelled out.) Display *Tues.* and ask the same series of questions. Conclude with: Months and days of the week use the first three or four letters of the original word in their abbreviations.

**Mt. Shasta**

**Tues.**

### STEP 4 ON THEIR OWN

Have students read each item in the first row below. Then have students match each abbreviation with the word that it stands for.

| | | | |
|---|---|---|---|
| **Slade Ave.** | **7.2 ft.** | **Nov. 8** | **Thurs.** |
| **November** | **Avenue** | **Thursday** | **feet** |

# Abbreviations



**CORRECTIVE FEEDBACK**

| | |
|---|---|
| **IF** students cannot recognize and read abbreviations, | **THEN** model recognizing and reading abbreviations, using Steps 2 and 3. Next, work through the Make It Easier activity. |

## Make It Easier

Students may benefit from focusing on abbreviations by type to help notice patterns.

- Many abbreviations for people's titles use the first and last letter of the word and end with a period. Display and read aloud the abbreviations. Then display the sentence, *Doctor Cate Lopez has a patient named Mister Tim Yang, Senior.* What words can we abbreviate? How can we rewrite the sentence with abbreviations? Record the sentence and read it aloud. (*Dr. Cate Lopez has a patient named Mr. Tim Yang, Sr.*)

**Dr. Mr.**

**Jr. Sr.**

- For place names, some abbreviations include the first and last letter with a period. Others include the first two or three letters and a period. Display and read aloud the abbreviations. Then display the sentence, *My address is Apartment 502, Hillside Road, Mount Clare.* Follow the same process as above.

**Ave. St. Rd. Ct.**
**Apt. Mt. Pl.**

- Continue the process with additional sentences.

## Make It Harder

Students who can recognize and read abbreviations can do an extension activity.

- Provide students with several street addresses, such as that of the school or of notable buildings or sites in the community. As an alternative, have students write several addresses of their own choosing. (Do not have students use their home addresses.) In these addresses, use abbreviations or direct students to do so.
- Have partners read the addresses aloud to each other, making sure that they say the abbreviated words just as if they were spelled out.
- Then have students write the words that the abbreviations stand for.

**SIDE A**

# Suffixes *-ful, -y, -ness*

A **suffix** is a group of letters added to the end of a word that changes the word's meaning, part of speech, or both.

**Connect to *myView Literacy:***
**Suffixes *-ful, -y, -ness:*** Unit 3, p. T152

**See digital practice on SavvasRealize.com.**

# ROUTINE

## STEP 1 INTRODUCE

Display the suffixes *-ful, -y,* and *-ness* on cards. These are suffixes. Adding a suffix to the end of a word creates a new word and changes the base word's meaning. Recognizing suffixes and learning their meanings can help you figure out the meanings of unfamiliar words.

**ful** | **y** | **ness**

## STEP 2 MODEL

- Display and review the meanings of the suffixes at the right.
- Display the word *help.* Slide the suffix *-ful* in place as you say: I know what *help* means. What did we just say that *-ful* means? (full of) So I can figure out that *helpful* means "full of help."
- Display *lace.* Slide the suffix *-y* in place as you say: I know what lace is. When I add the suffix *-y,* I can figure out that *lacy* means "having the character of lace."
- Repeat with the word *dizzy* and the suffix *-ness.* Conclude with: *Dizziness* means "the state of being dizzy."
- Note how some words change spelling when suffixes are added.

**-ful, -y** = "full of" or "having the character of"

**-ness** = "state or quality of"

**help helpful**

**lace lacy**

**dizzy dizziness**

## STEP 3 GUIDE PRACTICE

Display *fairness, prideful,* and *foggy*. For each word, ask: What is the word? What is its base word? What is its suffix? What does the suffix mean? What does the word mean?

## STEP 4 ON THEIR OWN

Have students add *-ful, -y,* or *-ness* to a word at the right to make a new word. Have them tell what the word means. Guide students as needed with new words, meanings, and spellings.

**waste** | **sharp**
**force** | **cloud**

**SIDE B**

# Suffixes *-ful, -y, -ness*

**WORD STUDY**
**GRADE 3**

## CORRECTIVE FEEDBACK

**IF** students cannot tell how the suffixes *-ful, -y,* and *-ness* change the meaning of a base word,

**THEN** model how each suffix changes a word's meaning, using Steps 2 and 3. Next, work through the Make It Easier activity.

## Make It Easier

Students may benefit from addressing words in explanatory sentences.

- Display the sentence. Underline each word part as you say: I see the word *hopeful;* it has a base word and a suffix: *-ful.* The suffix means "full of." What does *hopeful* mean? (full of hope) Underline the phrase. What is something that you are hopeful about?

  A person who is *hopeful* is full of hope.

- Display the sentence. Underline each word part as you say: I see the word *sandy;* it has a base word and a suffix: *-y.* The suffix means "full of" or "having the character of." What does *sandy* mean? (has the character of sand) Underline the phrase. What is something sandy?

  If something is *sandy,* it is full of sand or it has the character of sand.

- Continue as above. I see the word *dryness;* it has a base word and a suffix: *-ness.* The suffix means "the state or quality of." So what does *dryness* mean? (the state or quality of being dry) Underline the phrase. When might you check the dryness of something?

  If you check the *dryness* of something, you check its state or quality of being dry.

## Make It Harder

Students may enjoy an extension activity.

- Provide students with the following words:

| | | | | | |
|---|---|---|---|---|---|
| **risk** | **dull** | **doubt** | **moist** | **youth** | **lump** |

- Have students add the suffix *-ful, -y,* or *-ness* to each word and tell a partner what the new word means.
- Then have partners work together to write a sentence using each word.

SIDE A

# Vowel Teams *oo, ew, ue, ui, eu*

**WORD STUDY**
GRADE 3

**Vowel teams** are letter combinations that spell one vowel sound.

**Connect to *myView Literacy:***
**Vowel Teams *oo, ew, ue, ui, eu:***
Unit 3, p. T214

See digital practice on SavvasRealize.com.

## ROUTINE

### STEP 1 INTRODUCE

Display the vowel teams *oo, ew, ue, ui,* and *eu.* A vowel team is two letters that spell one vowel sound. Different vowel teams can spell the same sound. The same vowel team can also spell different sounds. Knowing the sounds for vowel teams can help you read new words. Today we will learn the different sounds that the vowel teams *oo, ew, ue, ui*, and *eu* can spell.

| | | |
|---|---|---|
| oo | ew | ue |
| ui | eu | |

### STEP 2 MODEL

- Display a two-column chart with the labels *cool* and *cue*. Read aloud the words.
- Display the words *stew, few*. I see that these words have the same vowel team, but they are pronounced differently.
- Listen for the vowel team sounds as I say the words: *stew, few. Stew* has the same vowel sound as *cool,* so I write it under *cool. Few* has the same vowel sound as *cue,* so I write it under *cue.*

| cool | cue |
|---|---|
| | |

### STEP 3 GUIDE PRACTICE

- Display the following words: *room, crew, clue, juice, feud, nephew,* and *argue.* Have students identify the vowel team in each word, pronounce the word, and add it to the chart.
- Afterward, read aloud the words and have students check to make sure each word is in the correct column.

### STEP 4 ON THEIR OWN

Provide students with word cards for the following words: *stool, fruit, blew, sleuth, blue, hue, knew,* and *value*. Have students read aloud and identify the vowel team in each word.

SIDE B

# Vowel Teams *oo, ew, ue, ui, eu*



**CORRECTIVE FEEDBACK**

**IF** students cannot correctly pronounce words with vowel teams *oo, ew, ue, ui,* and *eu*,

**THEN** model how to pronounce words with these vowel teams, using Steps 2 and 3. Next, work through the Make It Easier activity.

## Make It Easier

Students who cannot distinguish between the sounds vowel teams *oo, ew, ue, ui*, or *eu* spell make may need practice with listening for different vowel sounds.

- Listen for the different vowel sounds in these words. Say the words *cute* and *chute* and help students note the different pronunciations.
- Then say the word *suit.* Have students tell you the sound the vowel team makes. Does it sound like the vowel sound in *cute* or *chute?*
- Repeat with the following words: *tool, few, hue, fruit,* and *sleuth.*

## Make It Harder

Students who can pronounce words with vowel teams *oo, ew, ue, ui*, and *eu* may be ready to read multisyllable words that have these vowel teams.

- Have partners choose a familiar text. Then have them work together to look for multisyllable words that have the vowel teams *oo, ew, ue, ui,* and *eu.*
- When students find a word, have them read it aloud. Then have them add the word to a two-columned chart to show whether the vowel team spells the same sound as in *too* or *few.*
- Have students choose one word from each column and write a sentence using that word.

**WORD STUDY**
GRADE 3

**SIDE A**

# Irregular Plurals

An **irregular plural noun** is one that does not follow the usual pattern of adding *-s* or *-es* to form the plural. These irregular plurals may involve spelling changes or no change at all.

**Connect to *myView Literacy:***
**Irregular Plural Nouns*:*** Unit 3, p. T274

**See digital practice on SavvasRealize.com.**

# ROUTINE

## STEP 1 INTRODUCE

Have a dictionary available to confirm spellings. Irregular plural nouns do not follow the usual pattern of adding *-s* or *-es* to form the plural. Recognizing irregular plural nouns and their spellings can help you figure out word meanings and better understand what you read.

## STEP 2 MODEL

- Display *half* and *halves.* Usually we add an *s* or *es* to form a plural noun, but some nouns need a spelling change. Point to each word as you model forming the plural of *half* by changing the *f* to *v* before adding *es*.
- Display *mouse* and *mice.* Point to each word as you explain that, for some plurals, there is no rule. One *mouse,* many *mice.* Some nouns need a new word to form a plural.
- Display *sheep* and *sheep.* Some nouns do not change to form a plural.

| | |
|---|---|
| half | halves |
| mouse | mice |
| sheep | sheep |

## STEP 3 GUIDE PRACTICE

Display *child.* What word means "more than one child"? (*children*) Display *shelf.* How can I change the word to mean "more than one shelf"? (change the *f* to *v* and add *es: shelves*) Display *goose.* How should I change the spelling to form the plural? (change *oo* to *ee: geese*)

| | |
|---|---|
| child | shelf |
| goose | |

## STEP 4 ON THEIR OWN

Have students form the plural of each word. Have them write sentences using the singular and plural forms.

| | |
|---|---|
| woman | hoof |
| loaf | foot |

**SIDE B**

# Irregular Plurals

## CORRECTIVE FEEDBACK

**IF** students cannot recognize and form irregular plural nouns,

**THEN** model several examples again, using Steps 2 and 3. Next, work through the Make It Easier activity.

## Make It Easier

Students may benefit from practice with irregular plural nouns in context.

- Display *tooth, teeth,* and the sentences at the right. As you read each sentence, underline context clues that show whether a singular or plural noun makes sense. Do you brush one tooth or many? (many) Which noun is plural? (*teeth*) Do children lose one tooth at a time or many? (one) Which noun names one? (*tooth*)
- Display *wolf* and the sentence. As you read the sentence, underline context clues that show whether a singular or plural noun makes sense. Is a pack likely to be one wolf or many? (many) How can we form the plural of *wolf*? (change the *f* to *v* and add *es: wolves*)
- Display the sentences below. Have students fill in the blanks with the plural form of the words in parentheses.

  Five ____ worked together to paint the house. (man)
  A herd of ____ stood at the edge of the forest. (deer)

**tooth / teeth**

I brush my ____ every morning.

My little sister lost a baby ____ today.

**wolf**

A pack of ____ work together to care for their young.

## Make It Harder

Students who can recognize and form irregular plural nouns may enjoy an extension activity.

- Provide students with the following nouns: *thief, feet, moose, scarf.*
- Have students identify each word as singular, plural, or both. Then have them write sentences in which the usage of the noun is clear from the context.
- Have partners exchange sentences and revise to clarify the usage as needed.

**WORD STUDY**
GRADE 3

**SIDE A**

# *r*-Controlled Vowels *ir, er, ur, ear*

An ***r*-controlled vowel** refers to a vowel or vowel pattern followed by the letter *r* that has neither a long vowel sound nor a short vowel sound, but an *r*-controlled vowel sound.

**Connect to *myView Literacy:***
***r*-Controlled Vowels *ir, er, ur, ear:***
Unit 4, p. T22

**See digital practice on SavvasRealize.com.**

## ROUTINE

### STEP 1 INTRODUCE

An *r*-controlled vowel is a vowel or vowel pattern followed by the letter *r*. The *r* changes the sound of the vowel or vowel pattern to a sound that is neither long nor short. Today we are going to learn to read words that have the *r*-controlled vowel sound you hear in *burn*. Knowing how to read *r*-controlled vowels will help you read unfamiliar words.

| | |
|---|---|
| ir | er |
| ur | ear |

### STEP 2 MODEL

- Display and read aloud the word *firmly*. I hear the sound /ėr/ in the middle of *firmly*. Underline *ir*. The letters *ir* spell the sound /ėr/ in *firmly*. Blend the sounds to read the word *firmly*.
- Repeat for the remaining *r*-controlled vowel patterns using the words *serving, turnpike,* and *early*.

| | |
|---|---|
| firmly | turnpike |
| serving | early |

### STEP 3 GUIDE PRACTICE

- Display the word *thirsty*. Which *r*-controlled vowel pattern do you see? (*ir*) What sound does the vowel pattern spell? (/ėr/) Sweep your hand under *thirsty* as students blend the sounds to read the word with you.
- Repeat for these words: *person, curly,* and *learning*.

| | |
|---|---|
| thirsty | curly |
| person | learning |

### STEP 4 ON THEIR OWN

Display word cards for the following words and have students read aloud each word: *circus, jersey, hurting,* and *pearly*. Then have students use the words in sentences.

**SIDE B**

# *r*-Controlled Vowels *ir, er, ur, ear*

**CORRECTIVE FEEDBACK**

**IF** students cannot decode words with an *r*-controlled vowel or vowel pattern,

**THEN** model how to blend each sound-spelling in words, using Steps 2 and 3. Next, work through the Make It Easier activity.

## Make It Easier

Students who cannot blend the sounds in multisyllabic words with *r*-controlled vowels may benefit from practice with one-syllable words for each sound spelling.

- Display the word *fir.* Underline *ir* as you say: The *r*-controlled vowel sound in *fir* can be spelled *ir.* Have students blend the sounds to say the word with you.
- Have students underline the *r*-controlled vowel pattern in the following words: *stir, first,* and *chirp*. Then have students blend the sounds to read the words.
- Extend the activity by focusing on the other *r*-controlled patterns, one at a time.

## Make It Harder

Students who can read words with *r*-controlled vowels may enjoy writing rhyming words with *r*-controlled vowels.

- Have partners work together to create rhyming pairs of words that have different sound spellings, for example *fir/her.*
- After students complete their list, challenge them to write a poem that includes as many of the rhyming pairs as they can.

**SIDE A**

# VCCCV Pattern

**WORD STUDY**
GRADE 3

A **syllable** is a word part that has one vowel sound. Words with the syllable pattern VCCCV can be divided after the first or second consonant.

**Connect to *myView Literacy:***
**VCCCV Pattern:** Unit 4, p. T86

## ROUTINE

**See digital practice on SavvasRealize.com.**

### STEP 1 INTRODUCE

Review with students that words have different syllable patterns. Knowing where to divide words into syllables can help you read longer words. Today we will practice reading words with the VCCCV pattern.

### STEP 2 MODEL

- Words with the VCCCV pattern always have two consonants, a blend or a digraph, that stay together. Display the word *children.* Point out and underline the VCCCV pattern *ildre*. Then circle the consonant blend, *dr.* A VCCCV word divides between the blend or digraph and the other consonant, so I will divide the word between the consonant *l* and the consonant blend *dr*: chil/dren, *children.*

**children**

**chil / dren**

- Display the word *athlete.* Underline the VCCCV pattern. I see the VCCCV pattern in the word *athlete.* I also see the digraph *th.* I need to keep the digraph *th* together, so I will divide the word between the digraph *th* and the consonant *l*: ath/lete, *athlete.*

**athlete**

**ath / lete**

### STEP 3 GUIDE PRACTICE

- Display the word *sunshine.* What letters spell the VCCCV pattern? (*unshi*) What consonant blend or digraph do you see? (digraph *sh*) Where do we divide? (between *n* and *sh*) Divide the word. Read each syllable and then read the word. (sun/shine, *sunshine*)
- Repeat with the word *pumpkin.*

**sunshine**

**sun / shine**

**pumpkin**

**pump / kin**

### STEP 4 ON THEIR OWN

Have students identify the VCCCV pattern and the consonant blend or digraph in each of these words. Then have them divide the word into syllables, read each syllable, and then blend the syllables to read the word.

**hundred** **fishpole** **chestnut** **dolphin**

SIDE B

# VCCCV Pattern

## CORRECTIVE FEEDBACK

**IF** students have difficulty dividing words with the VCCCV pattern,

**THEN** model reading words with the VCCCV pattern again, using Steps 2 and 3. Next, work through the Make It Easier activity.

## Make It Easier

Students who cannot divide words with the VCCCV pattern might need more support with identifying consonant blends and digraphs.

- A consonant blend is two or three consonants together whose sounds are blended. Display *glide.* I see two consonants at the beginning of *glide: g, l.* The consonants *gl* form a consonant blend. I hear both sounds: /g/, /l/, but I blend the sounds as I pronounce the word. Say the word with me: *glide.*

  **glide**

- A consonant digraph is two consonants together that make only one sound. Display *reach.* I see two consonants at the end of *reach: c, h.* The consonants *ch* form a consonant digraph. I hear one sound: /ch/. Say the word with me: *reach.*

  **reach**

- Have students identify the consonant blend(s) or digraph(s) in each of these words. Then have them read the words.

  **shade** | **chair** | **plum** | **math** | **quick** | **stamp**

## Make It Harder

Provide an extension activity for students who can divide words with the VCCCV pattern.

- Provide word cards for the following words:

  **muskrat** | **anthem** | **inflate** | **chestnut** | **enchant**

- Have students divide and read each word. Then have them sort the words into two groups: VC/CCV and VCC/CV.
- Challenge students to find words in their reading to add to each group.

**SIDE A**

# Latin Suffixes *-able, -ible, -ation*

**WORD STUDY**
GRADE 3

A **suffix** is a group of letters added to the end of a word that changes the word's meaning, part of speech, or both.

**Connect to *myView Literacy:***
**Latin Suffixes:** Unit 4, p. T146

**See digital practice on SavvasRealize.com.**

## ROUTINE

### STEP 1 INTRODUCE

Display the suffixes. These suffixes go at the ends of verbs. When we add the suffix *-able* or *-ible* to a verb, we create an adjective. When we add *-ation* to a verb, we create a noun. Identifying suffixes can help you determine the meaning and part of speech of an unfamiliar word.

| able | ible | ation |
|---|---|---|

### STEP 2 MODEL

- Display the word *clickable.* I see a familiar base word: *click.* It's a verb—an action word. And I see a suffix: *-able.* Finding the parts of the word help me read the longer word: *clickable. Clickable* is an adjective—a describing word.
- Display *digestible* and examine its word parts, as above. Then add: The suffixes *-able* and *-ible* both mean "able" or "can be."
- Display *imagination.* I see another familiar base word, the verb *imagine.* And I see a suffix: *-ation.* This suffix means "the action or process of." I notice that the final *e* in *imagine* was dropped before the suffix was added. The new word *imagination* is a noun—a person, place, or thing.

clickable

digestible

imagination

### STEP 3 GUIDE PRACTICE

Display the word *teachable.* What is the base word? (*teach*) What is the suffix? (*-able*) What part of speech is *teachable?* (adjective) Now display *organization.* What is the base word? (*organize*) What is the suffix? (*-ation*) What is the part of speech? (noun)

teachable

organization

### STEP 4 ON THEIR OWN

Have students identify the base word and the suffix in each word and then identify the word's part of speech.

| sensible | curable | returnable | relaxation |
|---|---|---|---|

SIDE B

# Latin Suffixes *-able, -ible, -ation*

WORD STUDY
GRADE 3

### CORRECTIVE FEEDBACK

**IF** students cannot distinguish base words and suffixes and identify the new word's part of speech,

**THEN** model distinguishing base words and suffixes and identifying the part of speech, using Steps 2 and 3. Next, work through the Make It Easier activity.

## Make It Easier

Students who struggle to identify the meaning and part of speech for words with *-able, -ible,* and *-ation* may benefit from practice with the words in context.

- Display the sentences. Underline *bear* and *bearable.* In the first sentence, *bear* is used as a verb. Where do you see the base word *bear* in the second sentence? (in *bearable*) What is added to the base word? (the suffix *-able*) What part of speech is *bearable?* (adjective)
- Display the sentences. Underline *explore* and *exploration.* In the first sentence, *explore* is a verb. Where do you see the base word *explore* in the second sentence? (in *exploration*) What is added to the base word? (the suffix *-ation*) What part of speech is *exploration?* (noun)
- Display the sentences below. Have students identify the base word that appears in both sentences, identify the suffix, and name the part of speech.

  Can you flex your thumb? My thumb is quite flexible.
  The band can form many shapes. This formation is clever.

I cannot bear this cold weather.
This cold weather is not bearable.

We can explore this trail.
Our hike led to exploration.

## Make It Harder

Students who can distinguish base words and suffixes and identify parts of speech can do an extension activity.

- Provide students with the verbs at the right.
- Have students write a sentence using each verb. Then have them add *-able, -ible,* or *-ation* to the word and use the new word in a sentence.
- Have partners exchange sentences to check usage and spelling and to name the part of speech of the new words.

pose
exhale
force
starve

SIDE A

# Homographs



**Homographs** are words that are spelled the same but have different meanings and usually different pronunciations.

**Connect to *myView Literacy:***
**Homographs:** Unit 4, p. T210

**See digital practice on SavvasRealize.com.**

## ROUTINE

### STEP 1 INTRODUCE

Have a dictionary available to check pronunciations and meanings. Recognizing homographs and using the words around a homograph can help you figure out the meaning and pronunciation of a word.

### STEP 2 MODEL

- Display *present* divided into syllables. Point to each word as you say: Some words are spelled the same but have different meanings and pronunciations. *Pres/ent* with a short *e* sound in the first syllable means "gift." *Pre/sent* with a long *e* sound in the first syllable means "to share information with a group."

pres / ent

pre / sent

- Display the sentences. Model using context and a dictionary to determine the meanings and pronunciations of *bow*. I can look at the words around *b-o-w* to see which meaning is used and how to pronounce it. In the first sentence, *b-o-w* means "loops made with ribbon," so I pronounce it with a long *o* sound, *bow.* In the next sentence, *b-o-w* means "to bend at the waist," so I pronounce it with the sound /ou/, *bow.* Read aloud each sentence.

Tie the gift with a <u>bow</u>.
Actors <u>bow</u> after a show.

### STEP 3 GUIDE PRACTICE

Display the sentences. Which sentence is about a fish? (second) How do you pronounce *b-a-s-s* in that sentence? (with a short *a* sound) Which sentence is about a low and deep sound? (first) How do you pronounce *b-a-s-s* in that sentence? (with a long *a* sound) How can you check the meaning and pronunciation? (with a dictionary)

The song has too much <u>bass</u>.
Catch and release small <u>bass</u>.

### STEP 4 ON THEIR OWN

Have students determine two meanings and pronunciations for each word. Then have students use the words in sentences that reflect the meanings.

| | |
|---|---|
| wind | object |
| content | close |

SIDE B

# Homographs

**WORD STUDY**
**GRADE 3**

## CORRECTIVE FEEDBACK

**IF** students cannot use context to determine the meaning and pronunciation of a homograph,

**THEN** model the process again, using Steps 2 and 3. Next, work through the Make It Easier activity.

## Make It Easier

Students who cannot determine the meanings and pronunciations of homographs may benefit from experimenting with pronunciations in context.

- Display *lead* and the sentences. What are some ways to pronounce *l-e-a-d?* (with long *e,* /lēd/; short *e,* /led/) As you read each sentence, discuss clues that show the part of speech needed. What sentence needs an action? (first) Which pronunciation of *l-e-a-d* is an action? (/lēd/) How do you pronounce *l-e-a-d* to name a thing? (/led/) What sentence fits that word? (second)
- Display *desert* and the sentences. What are some ways to pronounce *d-e-s-e-r-t?* (des/ert, de/sert) As you read the sentences, discuss clues that show the part of speech needed. What sentence needs an action? (second) Which pronunciation is an action? (de/sert*)* How do you pronounce *d-e-s-e-r-t* to name a thing? (des/ert) What sentence fits that word? (first)
- Display the sentences below. Have partners fill in the blanks by reading aloud the correct homograph in parentheses.

  The ____ from my fall has almost healed. (wound)
  Please ____ the door when you leave. (close)

**lead**
____ the class to the bus.
Tools made of ____ are heavy.

**desert**
The sun beat down on the hot, dry ____.
The loyal dog would not ____ its home.

## Make It Harder

Students may enjoy an extension activity.

- Provide students with the following homographs: *contract, produce, subject.*
- Have students write sentences in which the meaning and pronunciation of the homograph is clear from the context.
- Have partners exchange sentences and revise to clarify the usage as needed.

SIDE A

# Homophones

**WORD STUDY**
GRADE 3

**Homophones** are words that have the same pronunciations but different spellings and meanings.

**Connect to *myView Literacy:***
**Homophones:** Unit 4, p. T276

**See digital practice on SavvasRealize.com.**

## ROUTINE

### STEP 1 INTRODUCE

Have a dictionary available to check spellings and meanings. Recognizing homophones can help you figure out word meanings and avoid confusion as you read.

### STEP 2 MODEL

- Display the sentence, pointing to *no* and *know* as you read it aloud. Say: *No* and *know* sound the same, but they have different spellings and meanings. I can learn the spelling of both words to be sure I use the correct word.
- Display the first set of words and the sentence. These words sound the same, but they have different meanings. An *eye* is a body part used to see. *I* is a pronoun that refers to me. Using the correct spellings completes the sentence in a way that makes sense: *I can close one eye to wink.* Write in the missing words.
- Follow a similar routine for the second set of words: *Two* is a number that makes sense in the first blank. The word *to* is often used with a verb like *share. We ordered two pizzas to share.*

We have no way to know if we do not ask!

eye I
___ can close one ___ to wink.

two to
We ordered ___ pizzas ___ share.

### STEP 3 GUIDE PRACTICE

Display the words and the sentence. What word is an adjective that can describe *books?* (*four*) What word connects *books* to the person they will go to? (*for*) Read aloud the sentence with students. *Dad found four books for me at the library.* Does that make sense? (yes)

for four
Dad found ___ books ___ me at the library.

### STEP 4 ON THEIR OWN

Have students define these sets of homophones and use the words in sentences: *break/brake; cell/sell; dear/deer; flour/flower.*

SIDE B

# Homophones



## CORRECTIVE FEEDBACK

**IF** students cannot identify and use the correct homophone,

**THEN** model the process to check the spelling of common homophones, using Steps 2 and 3. Next, work through the Make It Easier activity.

## Make It Easier

Students who struggle to use correct homophones may benefit from using the words in context.

- Display the homophones and the sentences. Guide students to identify the context in which each homophone is used. What does it mean to *buy* something? (to use money in exchange for a product) Which sentence(s) are about using money to get something? (first, third) What does it mean to be *by* something? (to be near it) Which homophone fits the second sentence? (*by*)
- Display and read aloud the sentences below. Follow the same process as above. Have students discuss the meanings of the homophones in parentheses and fill in the blanks with the correct homophone.

  Did you ____ the birds early this morning? (here/hear)
  The game will be ____ if everyone follows the rules. (fare/fair)

**buy / by**
Go to the market to ____ food.
Let's walk ____ the school.
I need to ____ boots before winter.

## Make It Harder

Students who can use homophones correctly may enjoy an extension activity.

- Provide students with the following homophones.

  **cent / scent** | **heel / heal** | **whole / hole**

- Have students write sentences or riddles using each set of homophones. For example, *Why could the skunk leave the store with some candy?* (*It had already left its scent*.)
- Encourage partners to exchange sentences and revise to clarify the usage as needed.

**SIDE A**

# Vowel Patterns *au, aw, al, augh, ough*

**Vowel patterns** are letter combinations that spell one vowel sound.

**Connect to *myView Literacy:***
**Vowel Patterns *au, aw, al, augh, ough:*** Unit 5, p. T22

## ROUTINE

**See digital practice on SavvasRealize.com.**

### STEP 1 INTRODUCE

Display the vowel patterns at the right. A vowel pattern is a combination of letters that spells one vowel sound. Different vowel patterns can spell the same sound. Knowing these vowel patterns can help you read words. Today we will learn the sound /ȯ/ that the vowel patterns *au, aw, al, augh,* and *ough* can spell.

au | aw | al | augh | ough

### STEP 2 MODEL

- Display the following words: *vault, paw, walk, taught,* and *bought.*
- Read aloud *vault*. Then underline the vowel pattern *au*. The vowel pattern *au* spells the vowel sound /ȯ/ in *vault.*
- Now I will read the other words. Listen for the sound the vowel patterns spell as I say the words. Repeat the process with the words *paw, walk, taught,* and *bought.*

vault | paw | walk | taught | bought

### STEP 3 GUIDE PRACTICE

Display the following words: *thaw, launch, talk, caught,* and *fought.* Have students underline the vowel pattern in each word and then read aloud the word.

### STEP 4 ON THEIR OWN

Provide students with word cards for the following words: *sauce, taut, saw, claw, walk, stalk, taught, caught, brought,* and *thought.* Have them read aloud each word. Then have them identify how the vowel sound /ȯ/ is spelled in each word.

SIDE B

# Vowel Patterns *au, aw, al, augh, ough*

**CORRECTIVE FEEDBACK**

**IF** students cannot decode words with the vowel patterns *au, aw, al, augh,* and *ough,*

**THEN** model how to decode words with these vowel patterns, using Steps 2 and 3. Next, work through the Make It Easier activity.

## Make It Easier

Students who cannot read words with vowel patterns *au, aw, al, augh,* and *ough* may benefit from practice with one pattern at a time.

- Display the word *claw.* Underline the vowel pattern *aw*. The vowel pattern *aw* spells the vowel sound /ȯ/ in the word *claw.*
- Have students blend the sounds to say the word with you.
- Repeat the procedure with the following words: *paw, straw,* and *draw*.
- Continue by focusing on vowel patterns *au, al, augh*, and *ough*, one at a time.

## Make It Harder

Students who can read words with vowel patterns *au, aw, al, augh*, and *ough* may be ready for an extension activity to find and use words from texts.

- Have partners make a chart with a column for each vowel pattern *au, aw, al, augh*, and *ough*.
- Then have students choose a familiar text. Have them work together to look for words that have the vowel patterns *au, aw, al, augh,* and *ough.*
- When students find a word, have them read it aloud. Then have them add the word to the appropriate column in their chart.
- Have partners use their words to create short rhymes.

**SIDE A**

# Vowel Patterns *ei, eigh*

**WORD STUDY**
GRADE 3

**Vowel patterns** are letter combinations that spell one vowel sound.

**Connect to *myView Literacy:***
**Vowel Patterns *ei, eigh:*** Unit 5, p. T88

**See digital practice on SavvasRealize.com.**

## ROUTINE

### STEP 1 INTRODUCE

Display the vowel patterns at the right. A vowel pattern is a combination of letters that spells one vowel sound. Different vowel patterns can spell the same sound. The same vowel pattern can also spell different sounds. Knowing the different sounds for these vowel patterns can help you read new words. Today we will learn the different sounds that the vowel teams *ei* and *eigh* can spell.

**ei**

**eigh**

### STEP 2 MODEL

- Display the following words: *veil, seize, weight,* and *height.* Underline the vowel pattern in each word.
- Read aloud *veil*. The vowel pattern *ei* can spell the long *a* sound in the word *veil.* Read aloud *seize*. The vowel pattern *ei* can also spell the long *e* sound in the word *seize.*
- Read aloud *weight*. The vowel pattern *eigh* can spell the long *a* sound in the word *weight.* Read aloud *height*. The vowel pattern *eigh* can also spell the long *i* sound in the word *height.*

**veil**

**seize**

**weight**

**height**

### STEP 3 GUIDE PRACTICE

Display the following words: *reins, protein, sleigh,* and *heighten.* Have students underline the vowel pattern in each word and read aloud the word.

### STEP 4 ON THEIR OWN

Provide students with word cards for the following words: *freight, neither, eight, reindeer, receive, neighbor,* and *beige.* Have students read aloud each word and identify the vowel pattern that spells the long *a,* long *e,* or long *i* sound.

SIDE B

# Vowel Patterns *ei, eigh*

**CORRECTIVE FEEDBACK**

**IF** students cannot read words with vowel patterns *ei* and *eigh,*

**THEN** model how to read words with these vowel patterns, using Steps 2 and 3. Next, work through the Make It Easier activity.

## Make It Easier

Students who cannot read words with the vowel patterns *ei* and *eigh* may need another way to identify the correct long vowel sound in words.

- Remind students that the vowel patterns *ei* and *eigh* can spell different long vowel sounds. When you read words with these patterns, you sometimes need to try out different long vowel sounds until you find the one that makes sense.
- Display the following sentence: *I weigh my dog on the scale.* Help students try out different long vowel sounds until they read aloud the word *weigh* correctly.
- Repeat with the following sentences and words:

  Mom marked my *height* on the wall.
  Blood flows in my *veins.*
  The moth flew up to the *ceiling*.

- Have students write lists of words by sound that they can use and add to as they encounter more *ei* and *eigh* words.

## Make It Harder

Students who can read words with the vowel patterns *ei* and *eigh* may be ready to write sentences with words that have these vowel patterns.

- Have students write as many words as they can for each of the vowel patterns *ei* and *eigh*. Then have them challenge a partner to read aloud the words they listed.
- Students can then write a sentence for words using each of the patterns.

**WORD STUDY**
GRADE 3

SIDE A

# Words with Suffix *-en*

A **suffix** is a group of letters added to the end of a word that changes the word's meaning, part of speech, or both.

**Connect to *myView Literacy:***
**Words with Suffix *-en:*** Unit 5, p. T146

**See digital practice on SavvasRealize.com.**

## ROUTINE

### STEP 1 INTRODUCE

Display the suffix. Many common words end with the suffix *-en,* which can signal a verb. Identifying word parts, meanings, and parts of speech can help you determine the meanings of longer words.

**en**

### STEP 2 MODEL

- Display *deepen* and the sentence. Underline the base word and then the suffix, as you say: I see a familiar adjective: *deep.* Then I see the suffix *-en.* The new word is the verb *deepen.* The *-en* suffix adds the meaning "to make or become" to the meaning of the adjective. So *deepen* means "to make or become deep."

  deepen
  I deepen the hole.

- Display *shaken* and the sentence. Underline each word part as you say: I see a base word: the verb *shake.* Then I see the *-en* suffix. Here, the word parts form the past participle *shaken.* Past participles mean "having been (something)." *Shaken* means "having been shook." Notice the spelling change. The final *e* of *shake* was dropped before the suffix *-en* was added.

  shaken
  He had shaken the box.

- Display *bitten*. Repeat as above. (*Bitten* means "having been bit.") Note that the base word's final consonant was doubled.

  **bitten**

### STEP 3 GUIDE PRACTICE

Display *sweeten.* What base word do you see? (*sweet*) What suffix is at the end? (*-en*) What meaning does *-en* add to the word? (to make or become) Was there a spelling change? (no) Repeat with *chosen,* but note the dropping of the final *e.*

**sweeten**

**chosen**

### STEP 4 ON THEIR OWN

For each word at the right, have students identify the base word, the suffix and its meaning, and any spelling rule used to add the suffix.

| | |
|---|---|
| tighten | hidden |
| spoken | thicken |

**SIDE B**

# Words with Suffix *-en*

**WORD STUDY**
**GRADE 3**

**CORRECTIVE FEEDBACK**

**IF** students cannot identify the base word and suffix and apply spelling rules,

**THEN** model identifying the base word and suffix and applying spelling rules to words with the suffix *-en,* using Steps 2 and 3. Next, work through the Make It Easier activity.

## Make It Easier

Students who cannot identify the base word and suffix and apply spelling rules may benefit from using the words in context.

- Display the first set of sentences. Underline *eat* and *eaten* as you say: In the first sentence, I see the verb *eat.* Where do you see the base word *eat* in the second sentence? (in *eaten*) What is added to the base word? (the suffix *-en*) Was there a spelling change? (no)
- Display the second set of sentences. Underline *ripe* and *ripen.* In the first sentence, I see the adjective *ripe.* Where do you see the base word *ripe* in the second sentence? (in *ripen*) What is added to the base word? (the suffix *-en*) Was there a spelling change? (Yes; the final *e* was dropped.)
- Display the sentences below. Have students locate the base word that occurs in both sentences, identify the suffix, and tell what spelling change occurred, if any.

  The air is fresh. Open the windows to freshen the house.
  The pond froze. We went ice skating after it had frozen.

I'll eat an apple.
Someone has eaten the apple.

This apple is not ripe.
It will ripen on the tree.

## Make It Harder

Challenge students to form words with the suffix *-en* and use them in sentences.

- Provide pairs with the following words: *forgot, damp, wove, straight.*
- Have individuals add the suffix *-en* to each word and write the new word.
- Have partners check each other's words and then work together to write a sentence using each word. Have them compare sentences with another pair.

SIDE A

# Schwa

**WORD STUDY**
GRADE 3

The **schwa** sound is the vowel sound in an unstressed syllable that is neither long nor short.

**Connect to *myView Literacy:***
**Schwa:** Unit 5, p. T206

**See digital practice on SavvasRealize.com.**

# ROUTINE

## STEP 1 INTRODUCE

In words with more than one syllable, some syllables are emphasized, or stressed, and some are unstressed. In many words, the vowel sound in an unstressed syllable is neither long nor short. It makes the sound /uh/. This is called the schwa sound.

## STEP 2 MODEL

- Display the word *away*. *Away.* The first syllable in *away* is unstressed. Underline the first syllable. The vowel sound of the letter *a* in the first syllable is not long or short. It is pronounced /uh/. /uh/ /wā'/, *away.* The first vowel *a* has the schwa sound.
- Display the word *lemon*. *Lemon.* The second syllable in *lemon* is unstressed. Underline the second syllable. The vowel sound of the letter *o* in the second syllable is not long or short. It has the schwa sound, /uh/. /Lem'/ /uhn/, *lemon.*
- Repeat with the words *camel*, *pencil*, and *album.* Point out that any vowel letter can have the schwa sound.

| | |
|---|---|
| away | a / way' |
| lemon | lem' / on |
| | cam' / el |
| | pen' / cil |
| | al' / bum |

## STEP 3 GUIDE PRACTICE

Display *balloon*. /Buh/ /loon'/. Which syllable is unstressed? (the first syllable) What is the vowel sound in the first syllable of *balloon?* (/uh/) What is that sound called? (schwa) Say the word. (*balloon*) Repeat with the words *problem, succeed, seven,* and *denim*.

balloon

## STEP 4 ON THEIR OWN

Distribute word cards with the following words. Have students use what they know about the schwa sound to read aloud each word. Then have them underline the syllable that has the schwa sound.

| | | | |
|---|---|---|---|
| nickel | alike | gallon | upon |

**SIDE B**

# Schwa

### CORRECTIVE FEEDBACK

**IF** students have difficulty reading words with the schwa vowel sound,

**THEN** model how to read words with the schwa sound again, using Steps 2 and 3. Next, work through the Make It Easier activity.

## Make It Easier

Students who cannot read words with the schwa vowel sound may benefit from reading only words with the schwa sound spelled with vowel *a* before moving on to other schwa spellings.

- Display the following words:

| | | | | | | |
|---|---|---|---|---|---|---|
| ago | panda | sofa | amaze | tuna | zebra | lagoon |

- Point to *ago*. Divide the word into syllables. Read each syllable and then read the word.
- Have students underline and read aloud the syllable that has the schwa sound. Then have them read aloud the whole word.
- Repeat with the remaining words.

ago
a / go
<u>a</u> / go

## Make It Harder

Have students who can read words with the schwa vowel sound identify the schwa sound in longer words.

- Tell students that the schwa vowel sound can occur in more than one syllable.
- Display the following words. Have students break each word into syllables, underline the syllables that have the schwa vowel sound, and then read aloud the words.

| | | | |
|---|---|---|---|
| **family**<br>(fam / <u>i</u> / ly) | **celebrate**<br>(cel / <u>e</u> / brate) | **festival**<br>(fes / <u>ti</u> / <u>val</u>) | **elephant**<br>(el / <u>e</u> / <u>phant</u>) |

SIDE A

# Final Stable Syllables *-le, -ture, -ive, -ize*

**WORD STUDY**
**GRADE 3**

Connect to *myView Literacy:*
**Final Stable Syllables *-le, -ture, -ive, -ize:*** Unit 5, p. T274

A **syllable** is a word part that has one vowel sound. A **final stable syllable** is a syllable that always appears at the end of a word.

## ROUTINE

See digital practice on SavvasRealize.com.

### STEP 1 INTRODUCE

The syllables *-le, -ture, -ive,* and *-ize* always appear at the end of a word. These syllables are called final stable syllables. Knowing how to identify these syllables can help us read unfamiliar words. Display these words.

candle | alive | picture | realize

### STEP 2 MODEL

- Point to the word *candle*. The final stable syllable *-le* always has a consonant before it. To read a word with the final stable syllable *-le,* we divide before the consonant. Divide the word, read each syllable, and then blend the syllables to read the word. Can/dle, *candle.*
- Point to the words *picture* and *realize.* To read a word with the final stable syllable *-ture* or *-ize,* we divide before the final stable syllable. Divide *picture.* Read each syllable and then blend the syllables to read the word. Repeat with *realize.*
- Display *alive* and *olive.* Final syllable *-ive* can have a long or short *i* sound. To read a word with the final stable syllable *-ive,* we either divide before the consonant in front of *-ive* or before *-ive*. Divide *alive.* Read each syllable and then the word. Repeat with *olive.*

can / dle

pic / ture

re / al / ize

a / live | ol / ive

### STEP 3 GUIDE PRACTICE

Point to *bundle*. What is the final stable syllable pattern? (consonant + *le*) How do we divide the word? (before consonant *d*) Read each syllable. (bun/dle) Now read the word. (*bundle*) Repeat with the remaining words.

bundle | structure | organize | active

### STEP 4 ON THEIR OWN

Have partners sort these words by final stable syllable and read the words: *thimble, dangle, texture, itemize, native, arrive, pasture.*

SIDE B

# Final Stable Syllables *-le, -ture, -ive, -ize*

## CORRECTIVE FEEDBACK

**IF** students have difficulty reading words with final stable syllables,

**THEN** model reading words with final stable syllables again, using Steps 2 and 3. Next, work through the Make It Easier activity.

## Make It Easier

Students who cannot read words with final stable syllables may benefit from practice reading words with the consonant + *-le* before moving on to other final stable syllables.

- Review that the final stable syllable *-le* always appears at the end of a word, and that a consonant always comes right before the *-le*. The final *e* is silent.
- Distribute word cards with these consonant + *le* words. Have students sort the words into groups by consonant + *le* syllables (e.g., *-ple, -dle, -gle*)
- Then have students read each group of words.

| C + *-le* | |
|---|---|
| apple | jungle |
| handle | angle |
| crumple | bundle |
| bugle | simple |
| paddle | bridle |

## Make It Harder

Students who can read words with final stable syllables may enjoy combining syllables to make words.

- Provide word cards for each of the following syllables.

| | | | |
|---|---|---|---|
| cra / dle | ol / ive | twin / kle | re / al / ize |
| nor / mal / ize | mois / ture | for / give | fu / ture |

- Mix up the cards and have partners combine two or three cards to create a word. Then have them write and read each word.
- Challenge students to come up with more words that end with final stable syllables.

# High-Frequency Words

*By critically analyzing classroom sight word lists, teachers can identify regularly spelled and temporarily irregularly spelled words that may be suitable for explicit graphophonemic instruction as opposed to whole-word reading and spelling approaches.*

—Katharine Pace Miles, Gregory B. Rubin, Selenid Gonzalez-Frey

"Rethinking Sight Words: The Interaction Between Students' Phonics Knowledge and Words' Spelling Regularity"

*The Reading Teacher,* Vol. 71, No. 6, May/June 2018

**SIDE A**

# Decodable High-Frequency Words

**High-frequency words** are the words that appear most often in our written language. **Decodable high-frequency words** are high-frequency words that have previously-learned sound-spelling patterns.

## ROUTINE

### STEP 1 INTRODUCE

Today, we will practice blending high-frequency words. Sometimes, we can blend these words using word parts that we already know.

### STEP 2 MODEL

- Display the word *north.* This is the word *north.* Use the word in a sentence. There is a park to the *north* of my house.
- Discuss the word parts that students may already know.
- Listen to the sounds as I read this word: /n/ /ôr/ /th/, *north.* Cover the word and spell it.

### STEP 3 GUIDE PRACTICE

- Discuss the parts of the word again. Let's blend and read the word together: /n/ /ôr/ /th/, *north.*
- Think about what the word *north* looks like. Use your finger to write *north* on your desk as you spell it: *n, o, r, t, h, north.*

### STEP 4 ON THEIR OWN

- Have students practice spelling the word *north*.
- Students should check their spelling and use the word in a sentence.
- Have students write the word on a card. They then practice reading and spelling the word three or four times.

**SIDE B**

# Decodable High-Frequency Words

## CORRECTIVE FEEDBACK

**IF** students cannot segment and blend decodable high-frequency words, **THEN** model how to segment and blend decodable words, using Steps 2 and 3. Next, work through the Make It Easier activity.

## Make It Easier

Students who cannot decode high-frequency words may use letter tiles to practice blending and segmenting words.

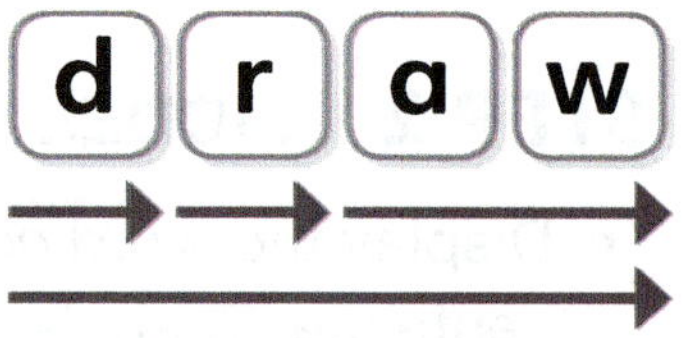


- Display the word *draw,* using letter tiles. Slide your finger under the word as you blend and read it. Listen carefully to the sounds. /d/ /r/ /ȯ/, *draw.* How many sounds do you hear? (*three*)
- Provide each student with a set of letter tiles. Spell the word *draw.* Slide your finger under each sound-spelling as we blend the word: /d/ /r/ /ȯ/, *draw.*
- Now write the word as you sound it out. Discuss the beginning, middle, and final sounds.
- Continue practicing with the following words.

| | | | |
|---|---|---|---|
| fact | stood | square | south |

## Make It Harder

Students who can decode high-frequency words may work with a partner to decode and spell more difficult words and use them in sentences.

- Create cards with the following words: *stood, square, decided, ready, produce, notice.*
- Each student chooses a card and uses letter tiles to spell the word. They scramble the letters from their word and pass the letters to their partner. The partner then unscrambles the word.
- Have students use each word in a sentence. Students then write the sentences.

**SIDE A**

# Non-Decodable High-Frequency Words

**High-frequency words** are the words that appear most often in our written language. **Non-decodable high-frequency words** are high-frequency words that do not follow a regular sound-spelling pattern *or* the sound-spelling patterns have not been previously learned.

## ROUTINE

### STEP 1 INTRODUCE

Today, we will practice reading irregular high-frequency words. These are words that do not follow a regular sound-spelling pattern.

### STEP 2 MODEL

- Display the word *heavy.* This is the word *heavy.* Use the word in a sentence. This watermelon is so *heavy! Heavy* is spelled: *h, e, a, v, y.*
- I'll look for word parts that we know. In *heavy,* /h/ is spelled *h* and /v/ is spelled *v.*
- Now I'll look for irregular word parts. I'll circle *ea* and *y* because in *heavy,* /e/ is spelled *ea* and /ē/ is spelled *y.*

### STEP 3 GUIDE PRACTICE

- Let's read the word together: *heavy.*
- Think about what the word *heavy* looks like as you write and spell *heavy: h, e, a, v, y, heavy.* Which word parts are irregular? (*ea, y*)

### STEP 4 ON THEIR OWN

- Have students practice spelling the word *heavy.* Write the word. Circle the irregular word parts. Discuss the order of the letters.
- Have students write the word again and use the word in a sentence.
- Students should practice reading and spelling the word three or four times.

SIDE B

# Non-Decodable High-Frequency Words

## CORRECTIVE FEEDBACK

**IF** students cannot read the non-decodable high-frequency words,

**THEN** model how to identify the regular and irregular sound-spelling patterns, using Steps 2 and 3. Next, work through the Make It Easier activity.

## Make It Easier

Students who cannot read non-decodable high-frequency words may use letter tiles and counters to practice reading and spelling words.

m o n e y

- Display the word *money*. This is the word *money: m, o, n, e, y.* I spent a lot of *money* at the store. Have students say and spell the word.
- Provide each student with a set of letter tiles. Spell *money*. Look for word parts that you know. Put counters under the irregular word parts. (*o, ey*). Discuss the irregular word parts.
- Write *money* as you spell it: *m, o, n, e, y.* Have students practice writing the word several times.
- Practice with the following words.

| half | built | ocean | front |
|---|---|---|---|

## Make It Harder

Students who can read non-decodable high-frequency words may work in pairs to read more difficult words.

- Create a set of word cards with the following words: *special, though, direction, government, material, language.*
- The first student flips a card and reads the word. The second student repeats it.
- Each student uses letter tiles to spell the word. Students take turns closing their eyes while the other student removes a letter from the word.
- Students guess the missing letter, write the word, and use it in a sentence.

# Syllable Patterns

*Students understand the challenges that come along with being unable to read words accurately and fluently. Increased skill in decoding multisyllabic words promotes students' continued development as proficient readers, as well as supporting their achievement into the upper elementary grades and beyond.*

—Dr. Jessica R. Toste, Kelly J. Williams, and Philip Capin

*Reading Big Words: Instructional Practices to Promote Multisyllabic Word Reading Fluency* (2016)

Intervention in School and Clinic 1–9 © Hammill Institute on Disabilities 2016

SIDE A

# Closed Syllables

A **closed syllable** is a syllable that ends with a consonant and usually has a short vowel.

## ROUTINE

See digital practice on SavvasRealize.com.

### STEP 1 INTRODUCE

Words are made up of syllables, and each syllable has one vowel. Closed syllables end in a consonant and usually have a short vowel sound. There are many words that you know with closed syllables—words such as *sun* and *fun*. Recognizing the closed syllable pattern can help you read longer words with two or more syllables.

### STEP 2 MODEL

- Display the word *dizziest.* The word *dizziest* has three syllables. Tap fingers to segment syllables: *diz* (tap), *zi* (tap), *est* (tap). Draw lines to divide the syllables. (diz/zi/est)
- The first syllable *diz-* is a closed syllable because it has the short vowel sound /i/ and ends with the consonant *z.* Underline *i* and circle *z.* The second and third syllables are not closed because *-zi-* ends in the vowel *i* and *-est* is an inflected ending. Repeat with *redness*.

**dizziest**

**redness**

### STEP 3 GUIDE PRACTICE

Display *retelling. Retelling* has three syllables. Tap fingers to segment: *re* (tap), *tell* (tap), *ing* (tap). Draw a line between syllables. (re/tell/ing) The first syllable *re-* ends in the vowel *e.* Is it closed? (no) Is the second syllable *-tell-* a closed syllable? (Yes, because it has the short vowel sound /e/ and ends in the consonant *l.*) The last syllable *-ing* is not a closed syllable; it is an inflected ending. Repeat with *unhappy*.

**retelling**

**unhappy**

### STEP 4 ON THEIR OWN

Draw a line between the syllables in each of the words at the right. Then, determine if each syllable is closed by underlining the vowel and circling the final consonant in each syllable.

**program**

**plentiful**

**jolliness**

SIDE B

# Closed Syllables



## CORRECTIVE FEEDBACK

**IF** students cannot identify closed syllables in multisyllabic words,

**THEN** model how to identify closed syllables in multisyllabic words, using Steps 2 and 3. Next, work through the Make It Easier activity.

## Make It Easier

Students who cannot identify closed syllables may benefit from a review of short vowels, as well as reading and sorting closed syllables using cards or tiles.

- Display vowels. There are five short vowel sounds in English. Point to each vowel and have students repeat the name and sound: *a, e, i, o, u.* Closed syllables usually have one short vowel sound and end in a consonant.

  **a, e, i, o, u**

- Display the word *velvet* using letter tiles. This is the word *velvet.* It has two syllables: *vel* (tap), *vet* (tap). Separate and display individual syllables. What is the vowel sound in the syllable *vel-?* (/e/) Does *vel-* end in a consonant? (Yes, the consonant *l.*) Then, *vel-* is a closed syllable because it has a short vowel and ends in a consonant. Underline the *e* and circle *l* in *vel-.* Is the syllable *-vet* closed? (Yes, because it has a short vowel and ends in a consonant.) Underline the vowel and circle the consonant. Repeat with *subject*.

  **velvet**

  **subject**

- Read and write these words. Draw lines to divide the syllables in each word. If the syllable is closed, then underline the short vowel and circle the final consonant.

  **misfit**

  **pretest**

  **lemon**

## Make It Harder

Students who can identify closed syllables can extend the activity by practicing with a partner.

- Students should find and write three multisyllabic words from classroom texts and then draw lines to segment each word into syllables.
- Partners should exchange lists and identify all the closed syllables in each word. Have students circle and read all the closed syllables.

SIDE A

# Open Syllables

An **open syllable** is a syllable that ends with a long vowel sound.

## ROUTINE

See digital practice on SavvasRealize.com.

### STEP 1 INTRODUCE

A syllable is a word part that has one vowel sound. Today we are going to focus on syllables that end with a long vowel sound, as in words such as *be* or *go*. These are called open syllables. Recognizing the open syllable pattern can help you read longer words with two or more syllables.

### STEP 2 MODEL

- Display the word *vacating*. The word *vacating* has three syllables. Tap fingers to segment syllables: *va* (tap), *cat* (tap), *ing* (tap). Draw a line to divide the syllables. (va/cat/ing)
- The first syllable *va-* is an open syllable because it ends in the long vowel sound /ā/ spelled *a*. Underline the *a* in the first syllable. The second syllable *-cat-* is not open because it ends in a consonant (*t*). The last syllable *-ing* is not open because it is an inflected ending. Repeat with *becoming*.

**vacating**

**becoming**

### STEP 3 GUIDE PRACTICE

Display *prevailing*. *Prevailing* has three syllables: *pre* (tap), *vail* (tap), *ing* (tap). Draw a line between syllables. The first syllable *pre-* ends in the long vowel /ē/. Is *pre-* an open syllable? (Yes, because it ends in a long vowel sound.) Underline *e*. Is the second syllable *-vail-* an open syllable? (No, because it ends in a consonant *l*.) The last syllable *-ing* is not open because *-ing* is an inflected ending. Repeat with *proponent*.

**prevailing**

**proponent**

### STEP 4 ON THEIR OWN

Draw a line between the syllables in each of the words at the right. Then, determine if each syllable is open by underlining any long vowels at the end of the syllable.

**reported**

**relaxing**

**politely**

**SIDE B**

# Open Syllables

### CORRECTIVE FEEDBACK

**IF** students cannot identify open syllables in multisyllabic words,

**THEN** model how to identify open syllables, using Steps 2 and 3. Next, work through the Make It Easier activity.

## Make It Easier

Students who cannot identify open syllables may benefit from a review of long vowels, as well as focusing on identifying open syllables in two-syllable words.

- Display vowels. There are five long vowel sounds in English. Point to each vowel and have students repeat the name and sound: *a:* /ā/, *e:* /ē/, *i:* /ī/, *o:* /ō/, and *u:* /ū/. Open syllables end in a long vowel sound.

ā, ē, ī, ō, ū

- Display the word *silent.* The word *silent* has two syllables: *si* (tap), *lent* (tap). Draw a line between the syllables. What is the vowel sound at the end of the first syllable *si-?* (ī). Then, *si-* is an open syllable because it ends in a long vowel sound. Underline the *i.* Is the last syllable *-lent* open? (No, because it ends in the consonant *t*.) Repeat with *paper*.

silent

paper

- Read and write these words. Draw lines to divide the syllables in each word. If the syllable is open, underline the long vowel at the end of the syllable.

equal

fancy

pretest

## Make It Harder

Students who can identify open syllables can extend the activity by practicing with a partner.

- Students should find and write three multisyllabic words from classroom texts.
- Partners then exchange lists and circle the open syllables in each word.
- Have partners read aloud the open syllables they circled.

SIDE A

# Closed and Open Syllables: Reading

Applying syllabication skills to reading leads to increased fluency and stronger comprehension.

## ROUTINE

See digital practice on SavvasRealize.com.

### STEP 1 INTRODUCE

Today we are going to use what we have learned about closed and open syllables to help us while we read.

### STEP 2 MODEL

- I am going to read this sentence. If I come to words I don't know, I will look for closed and open syllables to help me read the words. Read the sentence. Pause at *lizards.* I am not sure what this word is. I see the vowel *i* and the consonant *z* after the vowel. Sound out /liz/ with emphasis on the sound /i/ and the consonant *z*. *Liz-* is a closed syllable. This word is *lizards.* Continue reading.
- Pause at *giant.* I am not sure what this word is. I see the vowel *i,* but there is no consonant after it. I wonder if this word has an open syllable. Sound out /jī/ with emphasis on the sound /ī/. *Gi-* is an open syllable. This word is *giant.* Finish reading the sentence and then reread.

**We saw the lizards walk on a giant path.**

### STEP 3 GUIDE PRACTICE

Let's read this sentence together. If we come to words we don't know, we will pause and use our knowledge of closed and open syllables to help us read the words. Use the instruction in Step 2 to guide the students' reading of the sentence at the right. Pause at *victory* (closed syllable, *vic-*) and *remote* (open syllable, *re-*).

**Victory was mine when I found the remote on the couch.**

### STEP 4 ON THEIR OWN

Ask students to read the sentences at the right. Remind them to look for closed and open syllables to help them.

**The ambulance siren was loud.**

**Tam's dog looked at me in a distrustful manner.**

SIDE B

# Closed and Open Syllables: Reading

**SYLLABLE PATTERNS**
GRADE 3

### CORRECTIVE FEEDBACK

**IF** students cannot read multisyllabic words with closed and open syllables, **THEN** model how to read multisyllabic words with closed and open syllables in sentences, using Steps 2 and 3. Next, work through the Make It Easier activity.

## Make It Easier

Students who cannot read words with closed and open syllables may benefit from more explicit instruction on identifying open syllables.

- Display the word *predict.* Let's read this word together: *predict. Predict* begins with an open syllable, *pre-*. It is an open syllable because it ends with a long vowel sound, /ē/. Underline the vowel *e.* Let's say the open syllable together: *pre-*. Now, let's read the whole word together: *predict.*
- Display the word *notice.* Let's read this word together: *notice.* What is the first syllable in *notice?* (*no-*) Is *no-* a closed or an open syllable? (open) How do you know? (It is an open syllable because it ends with a long vowel sound, /ō/.) Underline the vowel *o.* Let's say the open syllable together: *no-*. Now, let's read the whole word together: *notice.*
- Repeat with the words at the right. Call on individual students to read the words. Then, ask students to identify the open syllable(s) in each word. Ask them to underline the open syllable(s).

**predict**

**notice**

**behind**

**decide**

**pho/to**

## Make It Harder

Students who can read words with closed and open syllables in sentences can enhance their practice by writing and reading extended sentences.

- Ask students to work with a partner. Each student should write a sentence with at least two multisyllabic words. One word should have a closed syllable. Another word should have an open syllable.
- Partners should exchange sentences and then take turns reading the sentences. Students should identify closed and open syllables in words.

SIDE A

# VC*e* Syllables

Syllables with the vowel-consonant-*e* (VC*e*) pattern have a long vowel and end with a silent *e*.

## ROUTINE

See digital practice on SavvasRealize.com.

### STEP 1 INTRODUCE

A syllable is a word part that has one vowel sound. Syllables with the VC*e* pattern have a long vowel sound and a final silent *e*.

### STEP 2 MODEL

- Display the word *immune*. This word *immune* has two syllables. Tap fingers to segment syllables: *im* (tap), *mune* (tap). Draw a line to divide the syllables. (im/mune)
- The first syllable *-im* is a closed syllable pattern because it has a short /i/ and ends in the consonant *m*. The second syllable *-mune* has the VC*e* pattern because it has the long vowel sound /ū/ and final silent *e*. Underline the *u* and circle the final *e* in *-mune*. Repeat with the word *explore*.

**immune**

**explore**

### STEP 3 GUIDE PRACTICE

Display *dislike*. *Dislike* has two syllables: *dis* (tap), *like* (tap). Draw a line between syllables. The first syllable *dis-* does not have a VC*e* syllable pattern. It has a short /i/ sound and ends in a consonant, so it is a closed syllable. Is the second syllable *-like* a VC*e* syllable? (Yes, because it has the long vowel sound /ī/ and ends in the silent *e*.) Underline the *i* and circle the final *e* in *-like*. Repeat with *unsafe*.

**dislike**

**unsafe**

### STEP 4 ON THEIR OWN

Draw a line between the syllables in each of the words at the right. Then, determine if each syllable has a VC*e* pattern by underlining the long vowel and circling the silent e at the end of the syllable.

**relocate**

**prideful**

**politeness**

SIDE B

# VC*e* Syllables

SYLLABLE PATTERNS
GRADE 3

**CORRECTIVE FEEDBACK**

**IF** students have difficulty reading or identifying VC*e* pattern syllables,

**THEN** model how to read VC*e* pattern syllables, using Steps 2 and 3. Next, work through the Make It Easier activity.

## Make It Easier

Students who cannot identify VC*e* pattern syllables may benefit from a review of long vowels and practice identifying the VC*e* pattern in monosyllabic words.

- Display vowels. There are five long vowel sounds in English. Point to each vowel and have students repeat the name and sound: *a*: /ā/, *e*: /ē/, *i*: /ī/, *o*: /ō/, and *u*: /ū/. Syllables with the pattern VC*e* have a long vowel sound and a final silent *e*.
- Display *kit*. The word *kit* has one syllable. The vowel in *kit* has a short /i/ sound. Add *e* to the end of *kit*. What is the new word? (*kite*) Underline the *i* and circle the *e*. When we add silent *e* to the end of *kit,* the vowel *i* has a long sound /ī/. In syllables that have the VC*e* pattern, the final *e* is silent. Repeat with *fin* and *fine*.
- Read and write the words at the right. Add a silent *e* to the end of each word to make the vowels long. Then, read the new words with the VC*e* pattern.

**ā, ē, ī, ō, ū**

**kit**

**kite**

**fin**

**fine**

**rob**

**not**

**sham**

## Make It Harder

Provide an extension activity for students who can identify and read words with the VC*e* pattern.

- Display the syllables at the right. The word is *incomplete*. Put these syllables in the correct order to spell the word.
- Give students the syllable parts below. Reorder these syllables and write the word. Circle the VC*e* syllable.

**com | in | plete**
(incomplete)

| | | |
|---|---|---|
| **e \| phone \| tel** | **gage \| ment \| en** | **lo \| cate \| dis** |
| (telephone) | (engagement) | (dislocate) |

SIDE A

# *r*-Controlled Vowel Syllables

An ***r*-controlled syllable** has a vowel or vowel pattern followed by the letter *r* that has neither a long nor a short vowel sound, but an *r*-controlled vowel sound.

## ROUTINE

See digital practice on SavvasRealize.com.

### STEP 1 INTRODUCE

An *r*-controlled syllable has a vowel or vowel pattern followed by the letter *r* that has neither a long nor a short vowel sound, but an *r*-controlled vowel sound. Today we are going to learn about syllables with the vowel patterns *ar, er, ir, or,* and *ur.*

| | |
|---|---|
| ar | er |
| ir | or |
| ur | |

### STEP 2 MODEL

- Display *jarring*. The word *jarring* has two syllables. Tap fingers to segment syllables: *jar* (tap), *ring* (tap).
- The first syllable *jar-* has the /är/ sound, with the vowel *a* followed by *r,* so it is an *r*-controlled syllable. Underline *ar.* The second syllable, *-ring,* is an inflected ending. Repeat with the word *hurtful.*

jarring

hurtful

### STEP 3 GUIDE PRACTICE

- Display *sorting. Sorting* has two syllables: *sort* (tap), *ing* (tap). Draw a line between syllables. Does the first syllable, *sort-*, have an *r*-controlled vowel pattern? (yes: *or*) Underline *or.* What sound does *or* in *sort-* make? (/ôr/) Does the second syllable, *-ing,* have an *r*-controlled vowel pattern? (No, it is an inflected ending.)
- Repeat with these words: *imposter* and *thirdly.*

sorting

imposter

thirdly

### STEP 4 ON THEIR OWN

Read each word aloud and draw a line between the syllables. Identify the syllables with the *r*-controlled vowel pattern by underlining the vowel + *r* in each *r*-controlled syllable.

important

targets

slurping

SIDE B

# *r*-Controlled Vowel Syllables

SYLLABLE PATTERNS
GRADE 3

**CORRECTIVE FEEDBACK**

**IF** students have difficulty identifying *r*-controlled vowel pattern syllables, **THEN** model how to read *r*-controlled vowel pattern syllables, using Steps 2 and 3. Next, work through the Make It Easier activity.

## Make It Easier

Students who cannot read the syllables in multisyllabic words with *r*-controlled vowels may benefit from practice with one-syllable words.

- Display the word *jar.* The word *jar* has one syllable. Underline *ar* as you say: The *r*-controlled vowel sound /är/ in *jar* can be spelled *ar.* Have students repeat the word and vowel sound /är/. Repeat with *stir.*

jar

stir

- Have students write the words below. Underline the *r*-controlled vowel pattern and then read the words aloud with a partner.

bird | surf | star | her | fork

## Make It Harder

Students who can read multisyllabic words with an *r*-controlled vowel pattern spelled *ar, er, or, ir,* or *ur* may be ready to write words with these *r*-controlled vowel patterns.

- Create lists of words for each of the *r*-controlled vowel patterns: *ar, er, or, ir,* and *ur.*
- Then, find a partner and take turns reading aloud the words on your list.
- Finally, write sentences using words with each of the *r*-controlled vowel patterns.

SYLLABLE PATTERNS
GRADE 3

SIDE A

# VC*e* and *r*-Controlled Vowel Syllables: Reading

Applying syllabication skills to reading leads to increased fluency and stronger comprehension.

## ROUTINE

See digital practice on SavvasRealize.com.

### STEP 1 INTRODUCE

Today we will use what we learned about vowel-consonant-*e*, or VC*e*, syllables and *r*-controlled vowel syllables to help us read.

### STEP 2 MODEL

- I am going to read this sentence. If I come to words I don't know, I will look for VC*e* and *r*-controlled vowel syllables to help me read the words. Read the sentence. Pause at *pancake.* I am not sure what this word is. I see the closed syllable *pan-,* but what is the second part of the word? I see the vowel *e* at the end of the word. Underline *e.* That means the letter *a* says the sound /ā/. The second syllable is *-cake.* This word is *pancake.* Continue reading.
- Pause at *under.* I am not sure what this word is. I see the closed syllable *un-,* but what is the second part of the word? I see the vowel *e* followed by the letter *r.* This means the second part of the word might be an *r*-controlled vowel syllable: *-der.* The second syllable is *-der.* This word is *under.* Finish reading the sentence and then reread.

**The pancake is under the pile of fruit.**

### STEP 3 GUIDE PRACTICE

Let's read this sentence together. If we come to words we don't know, we will pause and use our knowledge of VC*e* and *r*-controlled vowel syllables to help us read the words. Use the instruction in Step 2 to guide students' reading of the sentence at the right. Pause at *birthday* (*r*-controlled vowel, *birth-*), *surprise* (*r*-controlled vowel, *sur-;* VC*e, -prise*), and *excitement* (VC*e, -cite-*).

**Rex's birthday surprise led to excitement.**

### STEP 4 ON THEIR OWN

Ask students to read the sentences at the right. Remind them to look for VC*e* and *r*-controlled vowel syllables to help them.

**I saw the circus clown inflate the balloon.**

**That dresser is handmade.**

# VC*e* and *r*-Controlled Vowel Syllables: Reading



## CORRECTIVE FEEDBACK

**IF** students cannot read words with VC*e* and *r*-controlled vowel syllables in sentences,

**THEN** model how to read words with VC*e* and *r*-controlled vowel syllables, using Steps 2 and 3. Next, work through the Make It Easier activity.

## Make It Easier

Students who cannot read words with VC*e* and *r*-controlled vowel syllables may benefit from more explicit instruction on identifying VC*e* syllables in words.

- Display the word *lakefront.* Let's read this word together: *lakefront. Lakefront* begins with a VC*e* syllable, *lake-*. It is a VC*e* syllable because it ends with the vowel *e,* which makes the vowel *a* long: /ā/. Underline the vowels *a* and *e.* Let's say the VC*e* syllable together: *lake-*. Now, let's read the whole word together: *lakefront.*

lakefront

- Display the word *stovetop.* Let's read this word together: *stovetop.* What is the first syllable in *stovetop?* (*stove-*) Is *stove-* a VC*e* syllable? (yes) How do you know? (It is a VC*e* syllable because it ends with the vowel *e* that makes the vowel *o* long: /ō/) Underline the vowels *o* and *e.* Let's say the VC*e* syllable together: *stove-*. Now, let's read the whole word together: *stovetop.*

stovetop

- Repeat with the words at the right. Call on individual students to read the words. Then, ask students to identify the VC*e* syllable in each word. Ask them to underline the long vowel and vowel *e* in each word.

timeless
distaste
grateful

## Make It Harder

Students who can read words with VC*e* and *r*-controlled vowel syllables in sentences can enhance their practice by writing and reading extended sentences.

- Ask students to work with a partner. Each student should write a sentence with at least two multisyllabic words. One word should have a VC*e* syllable. Another word should have an *r*-controlled vowel syllable.
- Partners should exchange sentences and then take turns reading the sentences.

**SYLLABLE PATTERNS**
GRADE 3

**SIDE A**

# Vowel Team Syllables

**Vowel team syllables** have letter combinations that spell one vowel sound. A vowel team can represent a long, short, or diphthong vowel sound.

## ROUTINE

See digital practice on SavvasRealize.com.

### STEP 1 INTRODUCE

A vowel team is a syllable with two letters that spell one vowel sound. A vowel team syllable can have a long, short, or diphthong vowel sound. Different vowel teams can spell the same sound. The same vowel team can also spell different sounds. Recognizing the vowel team syllable patterns can help us read multisyllabic words.

### STEP 2 MODEL

- Display *sweetness.* The word *sweetness* has two syllables. Tap fingers to segment syllables: *sweet* (tap), *ness* (tap).
- The first syllable *sweet-* has the /ē/ sound, made by the vowel team *ee,* so it is a vowel team syllable. Underline *ee.* The second syllable *-ness* is a suffix. Repeat with the word *meaning.*

**sweetness**

**meaning**

### STEP 3 GUIDE PRACTICE

Display *dreaming. Dreaming* has two syllables: *dream* (tap), *ing* (tap). Draw a line between syllables. Does the first syllable *dream-* have a vowel team syllable pattern? (yes: *ea*) Underline the *ea.* What sound does the vowel team *ea* in *dream-* make? (/ē/) Does the second syllable *-ing* have a vowel team pattern? (No, it is an inflected ending.) Repeat with the word: *spoiler.*

**dreaming**

**spoiler**

### STEP 4 ON THEIR OWN

Read each word aloud and draw a line between the syllables. Identify the vowel team syllable pattern by underlining the two vowels in the vowel team.

**looked**

**loudest**

**painful**

**SIDE B**

# Vowel Team Syllables

**SYLLABLE PATTERNS**
**GRADE 3**

**CORRECTIVE FEEDBACK**

**IF** students have difficulty reading vowel team syllable patterns, **THEN** model how to read vowel team syllable patterns, using Steps 2 and 3. Next, work through the Make It Easier activity.

## Make It Easier

Students who cannot read the syllables in multisyllabic words with a vowel team pattern may benefit from practice with one-syllable words.

- Display the word *out*. The word *out* has one syllable. Underline the vowel team *ou* as you say: The vowel team *ou* in *out* says /ou/. Have students repeat the word and vowel sound /ou/. Repeat with *stool*.

**out**

**stool**

- Have students write the words below. Underline the two vowels in each word that make a vowel team, and then read the words aloud with a partner.

| | | | | | |
|---|---|---|---|---|---|
| flow | green | steam | plain | boot | tray |

## Make It Harder

Students who can identify and read multisyllabic words with a vowel team pattern may be ready to use the words in a sentence.

- Have partners choose a familiar text. Work together to look for words that have a vowel team pattern. When you find a word, write it down and read it aloud.
- Create a list of multisyllabic words with the vowel team syllable pattern.
- Finally, write three sentences using some of the words on your list.

**SYLLABLE PATTERNS**
GRADE 3

**SIDE A**

# Final Stable Syllable Consonant -*le*

A **final stable syllable** is a syllable that always appears at the end of a word. Syllables with a consonant plus the letters *l* and *e* always appear at the end of a word.

## ROUTINE

See digital practice on SavvasRealize.com.

### STEP 1 INTRODUCE

Syllables with a consonant plus the letters *l* and *e* always appear at the end of a word. For example, *candle* and *marble* both end in a consonant followed by the letters *l* and *e*. These syllables are called final stable syllables. Knowing how to identify these syllables can help us read multisyllabic words.

### STEP 2 MODEL

Display the word *candle.* The final stable syllable -*le* always has a consonant before it. To read a word with the final stable syllable -*le,* we segment the syllable before the consonant. Tap fingers to segment the word aloud: *can* (tap), *dle* (tap). Draw a line between syllables. The second syllable -*dle* is a final stable syllable because it has a consonant, *d,* plus *l* and *e.* Underline *dle.* The first syllable *can-* is a closed syllable because it has a short *a* and ends in a consonant, *n.* Repeat with *marble.*

candle

marble

### STEP 3 GUIDE PRACTICE

Display the word *rectangle. Rectangle* has three syllables: *rec* (tap), *tan* (tap), *gle* (tap). Draw a line between syllables. The final stable syllable always appears at the end of a word, so let's look at the last syllable, -*gle.* Does -*gle* have the final stable syllable pattern? (Yes, because it has the consonant *g* followed by *le.*) Underline *gle.* The first and second syllables, *rec-* and -*tan-,* are closed syllables. Repeat with *staple.*

rectangle

staple

### STEP 4 ON THEIR OWN

Read each word aloud and draw a line between the syllables. Identify the final stable syllable pattern by underlining the consonant, *l,* and *e* in the last syllable of each word.

pineapple

middle

reshuffle

SIDE B

# Final Stable Syllable Consonant *-le*



**CORRECTIVE FEEDBACK**

**IF** students have difficulty identifying or reading words with final stable syllables,

**THEN** model how to identify and read words with final stable syllables, using Steps 2 and 3. Next, work through the Make It Easier activity.

## Make It Easier

Students who cannot read or identify words with final stable syllables may benefit from an activity that will give them practice identifying and reading familiar words with the consonant *-le* pattern.

- Final stable syllables with a consonant *-le* pattern always appear at the end of a word. The consonant comes first and the final *e* is silent. Display the word *puzzle. Puzzle* has two syllables: *puz* (tap), *zle* (tap). The last syllable *-zle* is a final stable syllable because it has the consonant *z,* followed by *-le.* Underline *zle.*
- Provide partners with a set of the words at the right. Look at the last syllable in each word and sort the words into four groups by their consonant *-le* pattern: *-ple, -ble, -gle, -tle.* Then, read each group of words aloud to your partner.

**puzzle**

***-ple* / *-gle***

***-ble* / *-tle***

| | |
|---|---|
| jungle | bubble |
| people | cattle |
| little | trouble |
| goggle | sample |
| eagle | angle |

## Make It Harder

Students who can identify and read words with final stable syllables may enjoy combining syllables to make words.

- Provide each partner with a set of word cards with syllables below.
- Mix up the cards and lay them face down. Each partner should take turns picking one card. After you pick a card, read the syllable. Then add a consonant plus *-le* to create a new word. Write and read the new word. For example, if my card says *pic,* I can add the final stable syllable *-kle* to make *pickle.*

**pur | sim | brit | cir | wig | tri | gig | spar**

SIDE A

# Vowel Team and Consonant *-le* Syllables: Reading

SYLLABLE PATTERNS
GRADE 3

Applying syllabication skills to reading leads to increased fluency and stronger comprehension.

## ROUTINE

See digital practice on SavvasRealize.com.

### STEP 1 INTRODUCE

Today we are going to use what we have learned about vowel team syllables and consonant *-le* syllables to help us while we read.

### STEP 2 MODEL

- I am going to read this sentence. If I come to words I don't know, I will look for vowel team and consonant *-le* syllables to help me read the words. Read the sentence. Pause at *footprint.* I am not sure what this word is. I see the vowel team *oo.* Underline *oo.* The first syllable must be *foot-*. The second syllable is a closed syllable, *-print.* This word is *footprint.* Continue reading.
- Pause at *example.* I am not sure what this word is. I see the closed syllables *ex-* and *-am-,* but what is the third part of the word? I see the consonant *p* followed by *le.* The third syllable is *-ple.* This word is *example.* Finish reading the sentence and then reread.

**I used a footprint in my example.**

### STEP 3 GUIDE PRACTICE

- Let's read this sentence together. If we come to words we don't know, we will pause and use our knowledge of vowel team and consonant *-le* syllables to help us read the words. Use the instruction in Step 2 to guide the students' reading of the sentence at the right. Pause at *fewer* (vowel team *ew, few-*) and *puzzles* (consonant *-le, -zles*).

**Jess has fewer puzzles than Avis.**

### STEP 4 ON THEIR OWN

Ask students to read the sentences at the right. Remind them to look for vowel team and consonant *-le* syllables to help them.

**What is the venue for the obstacle course?**

**I read an article about suitcases.**

SIDE B

# Vowel Team and Consonant -*le* Syllables: Reading

SYLLABLE PATTERNS
GRADE 3

**CORRECTIVE FEEDBACK**

**IF** students cannot read words with vowel team and consonant -*le* syllables in sentences,

**THEN** model how to read words with vowel team and consonant -*le* syllables, using Steps 2 and 3. Next, work through the Make It Easier activity.

## Make It Easier

Students who cannot read words with vowel team and consonant -*le* syllables may benefit from more explicit instruction on identifying vowel teams in words.

- Display the word *bookmark.* Let's read this word together: *bookmark. Bookmark* begins with the syllable *book-.* The vowel team *oo* is in the syllable *book-.* Underline the vowel team *oo.* The second syllable is *-mark.* Let's say the second syllable together: *-mark.* Now, let's read the whole word together: *bookmark.*
- Display the word *value.* Let's read this word together: *value.* The first syllable in *value* is a closed syllable, *val-.* The second syllable has the vowel team *ue, -ue.* Underline the vowel team *ue.* Now, let's read the whole word together: *value.*
- Repeat with the words at the right. Call on individual students to read the words. Then, ask students to identify the vowel teams in each word. Ask them to underline the vowel teams.

**bookmark**

**value**

**chewing**

**recruit**

**sleuth**

## Make It Harder

Students who can read words with vowel team and consonant -*le* syllables in sentences can enhance their practice by writing and reading extended sentences.

- Ask students to work with a partner. Each student should write a sentence with at least two multisyllabic words. One word should have a vowel team syllable. Another word should have a consonant -*le* syllable.
- Partners should exchange sentences and then take turns reading the sentences.

# Vocabulary

*I don't think that there's one single way to teach vocabulary, but there is a stance toward teaching. What I'm saying is that you don't need a word list perspective but a word network perspective, and the networks can be morphological families.*

—Dr. Elfrieda Hiebert

CEO / President, TextProject

**VOCABULARY**
GRADE 3

SIDE A

# Oral Vocabulary: Build Background Knowledge

**Oral vocabulary** refers to words that we use in speaking or recognize in listening. When we **build background knowledge,** we make personal connections to texts.

**Connect to *myView Literacy:***
**Listening Comprehension:**
Unit 1, p. T16

## ROUTINE

### STEP 1 INTRODUCE

Choose words from a read-aloud text. Today we'll read [text title]. This [text or story] is about [topic]. While we read, we'll explore different words that will help us better understand the [text or story].

### STEP 2 MODEL

- Introduce the word. Listen as I say and write this word: *prodded.* Write *prodded.* What is the word?
- Provide a student-friendly definition and example. If you prodded someone, you encouraged someone to do something. You might prod your brother to help you dry the dishes.

### STEP 3 GUIDE PRACTICE

Guide students to connect the word to the story and their own knowledge. For example: *She prodded him for an answer.* Why? When have you prodded someone? Why? When are you more likely to prod: when someone is cooperating with you or when someone is not cooperating with you?

### STEP 4 ON THEIR OWN

- Review the example of the word from Step 2.
- Have students respond to the following prompt: *I prodded my friend when . . .* Check for students' understanding of word meaning as they share responses.

Choose words that
- are central to the story or text.
- are unusual and that students may not know.
- build knowledge.
- are worth knowing.

**SIDE B**

# Oral Vocabulary: Build Background Knowledge

**VOCABULARY**
**GRADE 3**

**CORRECTIVE FEEDBACK**

**IF** students have difficulty understanding the meaning of a vocabulary word,

**THEN** provide an additional definition or examples, using Steps 2 and 3. Next, work through the Make It Easier activity.

## Make It Easier

Students who struggle with word meanings may need more instruction during and after reading.

- Identify words that need additional review. Reread the text surrounding the word and guide students to use their background knowledge and experience.
- As you read, stop and discuss the meaning of the word. For example: What do you think *peeking* means? Explain the meaning of the word using the context of the story or text. Demonstrate *peeking* and ask students to share situations in which one might peek, based on their own experiences.
- After reading, have students draw a picture to illustrate the word. For example, for the word *peek,* they might show someone peeking around a corner. Ask students to share their drawing. You might peek out when you're hiding behind something. When else might you peek?
- Continue, discussing in a similar way words that students find challenging.

## Make It Harder

Students who understand the meanings of the words may extend their learning through one of the following activities.

- Ask students to identify and pantomime examples and non-examples of verbs and adverbs. For example: What would you do *carefully:* take a nap or balance on one leg? Act out the one you would do carefully. What else might you do carefully? What wouldn't you do carefully?
- Challenge partners to use the words in oral context sentences.
- If the oral vocabulary words center around a concept or theme, have partners make connections between the words.

**SIDE A**

# Use Resources

**VOCABULARY**
**GRADE 3**

Readers can use print or online **resources,** such as a dictionary, glossary, or **thesaurus,** to find the meanings of unfamiliar words.

**Connect to *myView Literacy:***
**Synonyms and Antonyms:**
Unit 1, p. T90

## ROUTINE

### STEP 1 INTRODUCE

A thesaurus lists words and their synonyms, or words with similar meanings. It can help you understand word meanings and shades of meaning among similar words to better understand what you read.

### STEP 2 MODEL

- Display and read the sentence at the right. Note the word *suspected.* What connotations, or associations, does this word have? (negative; related to questionable actions) Find synonyms in a thesaurus. Why did the author use *suspected* instead of *felt?* (It's more precise and shows Juan's feeling about the rabbits.)
- Display and read the sentence. Note the word *thrifty.* What connotations does *thrifty* have? (positive; careful with money) List synonyms from a thesaurus. How might the meaning change with the synonym *stingy?* (*Stingy* is negative. It may change readers' view of Bella.) What is a better synonym? (*frugal*)

Juan suspected that rabbits were nibbling the carrots in his garden again.

If I'm thrifty all year, thought Bella, I might be able to save enough money for a new bike.

### STEP 3 GUIDE PRACTICE

Display the sentence. Let's substitute a more precise word for *scared.* What should we do? (Check a thesaurus.) Guide students to look up *scared* and suggest a stronger synonym. (*terrified, petrified*)

Our dog was scared during the storm.

### STEP 4 ON THEIR OWN

Have students write sentences using the words at the right. Then ask them to look up the words in a thesaurus and rewrite their sentences with stronger or more precise synonyms.

| | |
|---|---|
| run | interesting |
| shout | funny |

**SIDE B**

# Use Resources

**VOCABULARY**
**GRADE 3**

## CORRECTIVE FEEDBACK

| | |
|---|---|
| **IF** students have difficulty using a thesaurus to help distinguish among synonyms, | **THEN** model the process, using Steps 2 and 3. Next, work through the Make It Easier activity. |

## Make It Easier

Students who struggle with using a thesaurus may benefit from reviewing synonyms and shades of meaning.

- Display and read the sentences at the right. Synonyms are words with similar meanings. Some synonyms have stronger or more precise meanings than others. In the first sentence, *loud* doesn't tell us very much. In the second sentence, *roaring* is a synonym for *loud,* but it is more interesting and precise, or exact.

> The crowd was loud.
> The crowd was roaring.
> **loud** *adj.* noisy, blaring, booming, roaring

- Display the sentence and the synonyms at the right. Which synonym might we substitute for *walk* in this sentence? How does this word change the sentence? (The synonym is stronger and more descriptive.) Repeat with similar examples.

> Let's walk up that hill.
> **synonyms:** stroll, step, hike, trudge

## Make It Harder

Students who are comfortable using a thesaurus can try this description activity.

- Ask students to write down eight to ten words that describe themselves, a place they enjoy, or a family pet.
- Have them exchange lists with a partner, and have the partner find synonyms for each descriptive word in a thesaurus. Remind them to consider the synonym's connotations, or associations, as well.
- Have students share their synonym lists and discuss whether the synonyms create a stronger or more precise description, and how.

VOCABULARY
GRADE 3

SIDE A

# Context Clues: Synonyms

**Context clues** are different types of hints, such as synonyms, antonyms, examples, or brief definitions, found within a text that help readers figure out the meaning of an unfamiliar word. **Synonyms** are words that have similar meanings.

**Connect to *myView Literacy:***
**Synonyms and Antonyms:** Unit 1, p. T90
**Context Clues:** Unit 1, p. T152

## ROUTINE

### STEP 1 INTRODUCE

When you don't know the meaning of a word in a sentence, you can look at nearby words for clues to its meaning. You may find a synonym for the word. Synonyms are words with similar meanings.

### STEP 2 MODEL

- This is how I figure out the meaning of an unfamiliar word. Display and read aloud the sentences at the right.
- I don't know the meaning of *investigate,* so I'll underline it. Then I'll think about the meanings of words I know in the sentences around it. Maybe the verb *explore* is a clue.
- I'll replace *investigate* with *explore* to see if it makes sense. It does! *Explore* and *investigate* must have similar meanings.

Let's investigate this cave. If we explore carefully, we're sure to find treasure—or at least bats.

### STEP 3 GUIDE PRACTICE

Display and read aloud the sentences. I don't know the meaning of *frequently.* What should I do? (think about the meanings of words I know) What word helps us understand the meaning of *frequently?* (*often*) Does *often* make sense in the first sentence? (yes) What is a synonym for *frequently?* (*often*)

"I frequently eat carrots," Gio said. "I have them so often that my skin is turning orange."

### STEP 4 ON THEIR OWN

Display and read aloud the sentences at the right. Have students find a synonym in the text to figure out the underlined word's meaning.

Let's not exclude anyone from the club. We don't want anyone to feel left out.

SIDE B

# Context Clues: Synonyms

VOCABULARY
GRADE 3

## CORRECTIVE FEEDBACK

**IF** students have difficulty finding a synonym to figure out the meaning of an unfamiliar word,

**THEN** model how to determine the meaning of an unfamiliar word, using Steps 2 and 3. Next, work through the Make It Easier activity.

## Make It Easier

Students who struggle with using synonyms to figure out meanings of unfamiliar words may need more instruction on the meaning of synonyms.

- Review with students that synonyms are words that have similar meanings.
- Say the word *afraid* and pantomime its meaning. What are some words or phrases that have a similar meaning? (*scared, worried, nervous*) Write a list of student responses. These are synonyms.
- Have students match the synonyms in the columns at the right. Then challenge pairs to take turns thinking of more synonyms for each set of words until they run out of ideas.

| | |
|---|---|
| rush | delicious |
| rest | hurry |
| difficult | relax |
| tasty | hard |

## Make It Harder

Students who can use synonyms to determine the meanings of unfamiliar words can challenge themselves to use synonyms in descriptive sentences.

- Have students form pairs. Provide or have students find an illustration or photograph of a place such as a desert, ocean, forest, or city. Ask one partner to share a sentence describing the place, using one of the adjectives at the right. Then have the other partner add another sentence to the description, using a synonym for the word.
- Challenge students to add more descriptive sentences using new adjectives and synonyms.

| | |
|---|---|
| calm | bright |
| dry | empty |
| crowded | peaceful |
| dark | |

SIDE A

# Context Clues: Antonyms

**Context clues** are different types of hints, such as synonyms, antonyms, examples, or brief definitions, found within a text that help readers figure out the meaning of an unfamiliar word. **Antonyms** are words that have opposite meanings.

**Connect to *myView Literacy:***
**Synonyms and Antonyms:** Unit 1, p. T90
**Context Clues:** Unit 1, p. T152

## ROUTINE

### STEP 1 INTRODUCE

When you don't know the meaning of a word in a sentence, look at nearby words for clues to its meaning. You may find an antonym for the unfamiliar word. Antonyms are words with opposite meanings.

> Signal words for antonyms:
> but — in contrast
> yet — however
> unlike

### STEP 2 MODEL

- This is how I use antonyms to figure out the meaning of an unfamiliar word. Display and read aloud the sentence at the right.
- I don't know the meaning of *significant,* so I'll think about the meanings of words I know in the sentence. The word *but* signals an antonym. Maybe *unimportant* is an antonym for *significant.* Then *significant* must mean *important.*
- I'll replace *significant* with *important* to see if it works. Yes!

> This clue is significant, but that one is unimportant.

> This clue is significant, but that one is unimportant.

### STEP 3 GUIDE PRACTICE

Display and read aloud the sentences at the right. I don't know the meaning of *recall.* What should I do? (think about the meanings of words I know in the sentence) What antonym helps us understand the meaning of *recall?* (*forget*) What signal word helps us identify the antonym? (*However*) What does *recall* mean? (remember)

> I can recall the story's beginning. However, I forget how it ends.

### STEP 4 ON THEIR OWN

Display and read aloud the sentence at the right. Have students find an antonym in the text to figure out the underlined word's meaning.

> In contrast to my cat, who rarely lets me pet her, my dog always wants affection.

SIDE B

# Context Clues: Antonyms

VOCABULARY
GRADE 3

## CORRECTIVE FEEDBACK

**IF** students have difficulty identifying an antonym to figure out the meaning of unfamiliar words,

**THEN** model how to determine the meaning of an unfamiliar word, using Steps 2 and 3. Next, work through the Make It Easier activity.

## Make It Easier

Students may need more instruction on the meaning of antonyms.

- Review with students that antonyms are words that have opposite meanings.
- Say the word *miserable* and pantomime its meaning. What words or phrases have the opposite meaning? (*happy, delighted, thrilled*) Write a list of student responses. These are antonyms.
- Display the words at the right. Have students match the words in the left column with their antonyms in the right column. Then ask students to think of more antonyms for each word in the right column.

| | |
|---|---|
| fail | terrible |
| distant | succeed |
| rapid | slow |
| wonderful | near |

## Make It Harder

Invite students to use antonyms to write sentences.

- Display the words at the right. Have students form pairs. Ask one partner to use the first word in the left column, along with an antonym for that word, to write a compare-and-contrast sentence about two people, animals, places, or things. For example: *I had a normal day at school, but Eugenia had an unusual day.* Tell students to include one of the signal words from the right column.
- Then have the other partner choose the next word and write a sentence following the process above. Have partners take turns for the remaining words.

| | |
|---|---|
| normal | but |
| peaceful | yet |
| great | however |
| delicious | unlike |
| difficult | in contrast |

**VOCABULARY**
GRADE 3

SIDE A

# Context Clues: Surrounding Text

Connect to *myView Literacy:*
**Context Clues:** Unit 1, p. T152

**Context clues** are different types of hints, such as synonyms, antonyms, examples, or brief definitions, within a text that help readers figure out the meaning of an unfamiliar word. **Surrounding text** includes the words and sentences near an unfamiliar word.

## ROUTINE

### STEP 1 INTRODUCE

When you don't know the meaning of a word in a sentence, you can look at the surrounding text for clues to its meaning. Surrounding text includes the words and sentences near an unfamiliar word.

### STEP 2 MODEL

This is how I use the surrounding text to figure out the meaning of an unfamiliar word. Display and read aloud the sentences at the right.

- I don't know what *ample* means. I'll look at nearby text for clues. The next sentence says, "We have more than enough to last until dinner." That tells me *ample* may mean "enough" or "plenty."
- I'll replace *ample* with *enough* to see if it makes sense. It does!

"I brought ample snacks for our hike," Raven said. "We have more than enough to last until dinner."

### STEP 3 GUIDE PRACTICE

Display and read aloud the sentence at the right. I don't know what *phobia* means. What should I do? (look at the surrounding text) What text helps show the meaning of *phobia*? (*strong fear*) What does *phobia* mean? (fear of something)

People who have a phobia, or strong fear, of cats hide when they see one.

### STEP 4 ON THEIR OWN

Display and read aloud the sentences at the right. Have students use the surrounding text to figure out the underlined word's meaning.

That film has flaws. The plot is bad, and the acting is even worse.

SIDE B

# Context Clues: Surrounding Text

VOCABULARY
GRADE 3

**CORRECTIVE FEEDBACK**

**IF** students cannot use surrounding text to figure out the meanings of unfamiliar words,

**THEN** model how to determine the meaning of an unfamiliar word, using Steps 2 and 3. Next, work through the Make It Easier activity.

## Make It Easier

Students who struggle with using surrounding text as context clues may benefit from learning to identify types of surrounding text that offer clues to meaning.

- Review with students that context clues are words that give hints to the meaning of an unfamiliar word. These clues may include explanations, definitions, and examples.
- Say the word *clumsy* and pantomime its meaning. What are examples of something someone who is clumsy might do? Use one response to write and display context sentences. (For example, *Sometimes I'm clumsy. I trip over my own feet a lot!*) Ask students which part of the text gives an example that shows the meaning of *clumsy*.
- Repeat the exercise, using the words *comfortable* and *feline.* Pantomime or show images to share the words' meanings. For *comfortable,* ask students to give an explanation or example. For *feline,* ask them to give a definition. Use responses to write and display context sentences. Have students point out the context clues.

## Make It Harder

Challenge students to write their own context sentences. Provide a dictionary for students to use as needed.

- Display the words at the right. Have students form pairs. Ask one partner to use the first word to write one or two sentences that include a context clue in the surrounding text. The clue should be an explanation, definition, or example. Then have the other partner use the same word to write a context sentence(s) including one of the other clue types.
- Challenge students to use all three clue types for each word.

sequence
fossil
rapid

SIDE A

# Word Parts for Meaning

**VOCABULARY**
GRADE 3

**Word parts** are base words, roots, prefixes, and suffixes with specific meanings that contribute to the meaning of a word as a whole.

**Connect to *myView Literacy:***
**Related Words:** Unit 1, p. T20

## ROUTINE

### STEP 1 INTRODUCE

Long words may be hard to read. Looking at word parts, such as base words, roots, prefixes, and suffixes, can help you figure out the meanings of longer words.

### STEP 2 MODEL

- Display and read aloud the word *declaration*. I know the verb *declare*. It means "to say something in a public, official way." *Declaration* probably is related to *declare*. Underline *declar*.
- I also recognize the suffix *-tion*. It turns a word into a noun. Underline *-tion*. The word parts *declar* and *-tion* help me figure out that a declaration is a public, official statement.
- Repeat the exercise with a compound word (such as *wildfire*) and related words containing Greek or Latin roots (such as *thermometer* and *thermostat*).

declaration
declaration
declaration

### STEP 3 GUIDE PRACTICE

Display and read the word *disagree*. If I don't know this word's meaning, what should I do? (look for word parts) What base word is in *disagree?* (agree) What prefix is in *disagree?* (*dis-*) *Dis-* means "not." What does *disagree* probably mean? (not agree)

disagree
disagree
disagree

### STEP 4 ON THEIR OWN

Have students identify the word parts in each word and then figure out the word's meaning. Offer word-part definitions as needed.

| outerwear | preapprove | impossibly | sleepiness |
|---|---|---|---|

SIDE B
# Word Parts for Meaning

### CORRECTIVE FEEDBACK

**IF** students cannot use base words, roots, and affixes to determine word meanings,

**THEN** model identifying word parts and using them to determine meanings, using Steps 2 and 3. Next, work through the Make It Easier activity.

## Make It Easier

Students who struggle with using word parts to determine the meanings of unfamiliar words may need help identifying word parts and understanding what different affixes mean.

- Display and say the word *plainness*. Cover one part of the word as you ask students to identify the other part. In the word *plainness,* one word part is *plain*. *Plain* is a base word. It's an adjective that means "simple" or "ordinary." The other word part is *-ness*. It's a suffix that turns a word into a noun. Ask students to determine the word's meaning.
- Repeat the exercise with the words *nonfiction, predict,* and *moonbeam*. You may wish to offer sentence frames such as the following: *Nonfiction* has ______ word parts. The base word is ______. It means "a made-up story." The other word part is ______. It's a prefix that means "not." This tells me that *nonfiction* probably means ______. Clarify the meanings of any unfamiliar prefixes or suffixes.

## Make It Harder

Have students who can use word parts to determine word meanings experiment with making up words using word parts and then checking to see if they are real words.

- Provide word-part cards that show one word part on each card. Include base words: *sharp, grace, kind, like, perfect;* roots: *dict, cred;* prefixes: *pre-, dis-, in-, im-;* and suffixes: *-ful, -ness, -en, -ible*.
- Ask students to put together two or more word-part cards to make words and predict the words' meanings. Ask them to check a dictionary to make sure that their words exist and their definitions are on target.
- Challenge students to use their words in context sentences.

**VOCABULARY**
GRADE 3

SIDE A

# Figurative Language: Similes

**Figurative language** gives words a meaning beyond their dictionary definition. A **simile** is a type of figurative language that compares two things using *like* or *as*.

**Connect to *myView Literacy:***
**Describe Figurative Language:**
Unit 1, p. T60

## ROUTINE

### STEP 1 INTRODUCE

Similes are a kind of figurative language. They compare two things using *like* or *as*. To understand a simile, you can think about the things being compared, how they are similar, and how the simile connects to the text. Understanding similes helps you better understand the text.

### STEP 2 MODEL

- This is how I can recognize and understand a simile. Display and read aloud the sentence at the right.
- I can tell this sentence contains a simile because it compares two things—a person and a sheet—using the word *as*.
- Sheets are often white. Comparing Ari to a sheet means he was extremely pale. That makes sense with the text. People sometimes turn very pale when they're scared.

After watching the scary movie, Ari looked as pale as a sheet.

### STEP 3 GUIDE PRACTICE

Display and read the sentence at the right. What is the simile? ("like a tiger stalking its prey") What two things are being compared? (Fluffy and a tiger) Which word signals a simile? (*like*) What does the simile mean? (When cats play or hunt, they act like tigers.)

Fluffy crept up on her toy mouse like a tiger stalking its prey.

### STEP 4 ON THEIR OWN

Display and read aloud the sentence at the right. Have students underline the simile and tell what is being compared and why.

The ocean waves towered like a vast blue mountain range.

**SIDE B**

# Figurative Language: Similes

**VOCABULARY**
**GRADE 3**

**CORRECTIVE FEEDBACK**

**IF** students cannot identify and understand similes, | **THEN** model the process, using Steps 2 and 3. Next, work through the Make It Easier activity.

## Make It Easier

Students may benefit from practice distinguishing literal and figurative language.

- Review literal and figurative language. Literal language means exactly what it says. In figurative language, such as similes, the meaning is different from the basic meaning of the words.
- Write and display the sentence at the right. Draw or show an image of a pancake and a bike with a flat tire. Ask: Is a flat tire really the same as a pancake? Explain that the sentence uses figurative language. Underline the word *as,* and note that similes always include the word *like* or *as.*
- Note that a simile compares two unlike things that are similar in some way. How are a flat tire and a pancake alike?
- Offer more sentences with similes. Have students identify and draw the things being compared, underline *like* or *as,* and discuss how the things are similar.

My bike tire is as flat as a pancake.

## Make It Harder

Challenge students to complete a simile-filled story.

- Have students form pairs. Ask one partner to fill in the blank to complete the first sentence at the right. Then have the second partner complete the next sentence.
- Have partners take turns completing the sentences. Then challenge them to add more sentences to the story, using a simile in each one.

As I stood on the diving board, I was shaking like a ______. The pool below looked as distant as ______. The crowd's cheers were as loud as ______. I dived into the water like a ______.

SIDE A

# Figurative Language: Metaphors

**VOCABULARY**
GRADE 3

**Connect to *myView Literacy:***
**Possible Teaching Point:**
Unit 1, p. T236

**Figurative language** gives words a meaning beyond their dictionary definition. A **metaphor** is a type of figurative language that makes a comparison between unlike things without using *like* or *as*.

## ROUTINE

### STEP 1 INTRODUCE

Metaphors are a kind of figurative language. They compare two unlike things, saying one thing is another. To understand metaphors, you can think about the two things being compared, how they are similar, and how the metaphor connects to the text.

### STEP 2 MODEL

- This is how I can recognize and understand a metaphor. Display and read aloud the sentence at the right.
- I can tell this sentence contains a metaphor because it compares two things—legs and noodles—by saying one is the other.
- Overcooked noodles are limp and lifeless. Comparing Tanya's legs to noodles means they are tired and weak. That makes sense. Legs often feel weak after a race.

By the end of the race, Tanya's legs are overcooked noodles.

### STEP 3 GUIDE PRACTICE

Display and read the sentence at the right. What is the metaphor? ("this room is Antarctica") What two things are being compared? (a room and Antarctica) What does the metaphor mean? (The room is very cold, like the ice-covered continent Antarctica.)

I have to find a sweater because this room is Antarctica.

### STEP 4 ON THEIR OWN

Display and read aloud the sentence at the right. Have students underline the metaphor and tell what is being compared and why.

My strange dream was a jigsaw puzzle with many missing pieces.

SIDE B

# Figurative Language: Metaphors

## CORRECTIVE FEEDBACK

**IF** students cannot identify and understand metaphors, **THEN** model the process, using Steps 2 and 3. Next, work through the Make It Easier activity.

## Make It Easier

Students may benefit from more practice distinguishing literal and figurative language.

- Review literal and figurative language. Literal language means exactly what it says. In figurative language, such as metaphors, the meaning is different from the basic meaning of the words.
- Write and display the sentence at the right. Ask: Is a computer really a dinosaur? Explain that the sentence uses figurative language. Underline *Our computer is a dinosaur,* and explain that it is a metaphor. A metaphor compares two things by saying one thing is another thing.
- Note that a metaphor compares two unlike things that are similar in some way. How might a dinosaur be like a computer that needs to be replaced?
- Offer more sentences containing metaphors. Invite students to identify and draw the things being compared. Discuss how the things are alike.

Our computer is a dinosaur, and we should have replaced it years ago.

## Make It Harder

Have students write a descriptive paragraph using their own metaphors.

- Display the words at the right. Ask pairs of students to work together to write a description of a day in nature. Have them start by making metaphors from the words shown, pairing a word from the left column with a phrase from the right column.
- Challenge students to add metaphors to their paragraph and explain how their comparisons make sense.

| | |
|---|---|
| sun | silver mirror |
| wind | fluffy sheep |
| lake | gold coin |
| clouds | howling wolf |

**SIDE A**

# Figurative Language: Analogies

**VOCABULARY**
GRADE 3

**Figurative language** gives words a meaning beyond their dictionary definition. An **analogy** is a type of figurative language that compares something unknown to something familiar.

**Connect to *myView Literacy:***
**Analogies:** Unit 4, p. T208

## ROUTINE

### STEP 1 INTRODUCE

Analogies are a kind of figurative language. They compare pairs of items that have something in common. To finish an analogy, think about how each pair of words is connected.

### STEP 2 MODEL

- This is how I can complete an analogy. Display and read aloud the text at the right.
- First, I'll figure out the relationship between the first word pair, *slither* and *snake*. A snake slithers when it moves. Maybe the relationship is how animals move.
- The next word is *waddle*. What moves by waddling? A duck! Display the completed analogy. Slither is to snake as waddle is to duck—that makes sense.

Slither is to snake as waddle is to ________.

Slither is to snake as waddle is to duck.

### STEP 3 GUIDE PRACTICE

Display and read the analogy at the right. What is compared in the first part? (*hard* and *soft*) What is the relationship? (opposites) How should *bumpy* relate to the missing word? (opposites) What word fits? (*smooth, flat*)

Hard is to soft as bumpy is to ______.

### STEP 4 ON THEIR OWN

Display and read aloud the analogy at the right. Have students underline the items being compared, explain their relationship, and fill in the blank.

Milk is to cows as eggs are to ________.

SIDE B

# Figurative Language: Analogies

**VOCABULARY**
**GRADE 3**

## CORRECTIVE FEEDBACK

**IF** students cannot understand and complete analogies,

**THEN** model the process, using Steps 2 and 3. Next, work through the Make It Easier activity.

## Make It Easier

Students who struggle to understand and complete analogies may need help identifying different types of relationships between words.

- Display and say the words *tiny* and *little.* What's the relationship between these words? If something is *tiny,* you can also describe it as *little. Tiny* and *little* have the same, or almost the same, meaning. That's how they are related. Display and say the words *tiny* and *huge.* What's the relationship between these words? Something *tiny* is not at all *huge.* The words are opposites. That's how they are related.
- Ask students to find the relationships between the other word pairs at the right. You may wish to offer sentence frames such as the following: A kitten is a ______ cat, and a puppy is a _____ dog. A lid is the _____ of a jar, and a roof is the _____ of a house.

| | |
|---|---|
| tiny | little |
| tiny | huge |

| | |
|---|---|
| kitten | cat |
| puppy | dog |
| lid | jar |
| roof | house |

## Make It Harder

Students can create their own analogies for a partner to complete.

- Have one partner use a word pair at the right to form the start of an analogy. That partner should think of the first word for the second part of the analogy. Then have the other partner finish the analogy. (For example, the first partner might say, *Rain is to drops as snow is to _____.*)
- Partners can take turns starting and finishing the analogies. Challenge pairs to come up with original analogies.

| | |
|---|---|
| rain | drops |
| plus | add |
| circle | shape |
| fast | quick |
| goal | soccer |

# Fluency

- Self-Monitor Fluency

*Reading fluency—reading with accuracy, automaticity, and prosody—also serves as a bridge between decoding and reading comprehension. Reading words accurately supports comprehension because it helps readers build an accurate base understanding of the text. Reading words with automaticity allows readers to devote more cognitive attention to comprehension. Reading with prosody (e.g., appropriate expression, phrasing) both reflects and supports comprehension.*

—Nell K. Duke, Alessandra E. Ward, P. David Pearson

"The Science of Reading Comprehension Instruction"

*The Reading Teacher*, Vol. 74, No. 6, May/June 2021

SIDE A

# Accuracy

FLUENCY
GRADE 3

**Accuracy** refers to reading a text correctly, without omitting, adding, or changing any of the words.

**Connect to *myView Literacy:***
**Fluency:** Unit 1, p. T56

## ROUTINE

### STEP 1 INTRODUCE

Describe the skill. Reading accurately means that we read all words correctly. We don't skip words, add words, or change the order of the words. We read accurately so that we understand exactly what the author wrote.

### STEP 2 MODEL

- Display a text and model reading aloud the first part.
- Follow along and listen to hear if I read every word. Model reading aloud the same section of text a second time. Model self-correcting.
- Then ask questions, such as, *Did I read all the words accurately? Did I skip or add any words? Did I read the words in the correct order?*

### STEP 3 GUIDE PRACTICE

- Discuss what the text is about to clarify any potential misunderstandings.
- Distribute a copy of the same text to each student. Point out the punctuation marks and remind students to pause when they come to a comma and stop for a moment when they come to a period.
- Let's read the text aloud together. Let's read all the words exactly as they appear. Good readers read all the words correctly, at a speed that is not too fast and not too slow. They self-correct if they misread a word. Read aloud the same text.

### STEP 4 ON THEIR OWN

- Now that we've read aloud together, let's practice reading aloud with a partner. Have pairs read aloud the rest of the text to each other, taking turns with each paragraph.
- For optimal fluency, have students read the text aloud a few times.
- If you realize you've made a mistake as you're reading, remember that it's okay to correct yourself. Provide feedback on students' accuracy and their ability to self-correct.

SIDE B

# Accuracy

**CORRECTIVE FEEDBACK**

**IF** students have difficulty reading aloud with accuracy, | **THEN** model how to read accurately, using Steps 2 and 3. Next, work through the Make It Easier activity.

## Make It Easier

Ensure that students who make errors while reading aloud have ample opportunity to practice reading aloud and listening to fluent oral readers.

- Evaluate each student's errors and determine whether additional instruction in decoding, vocabulary, or comprehension strategies might be needed.
- If reading too quickly is causing omissions, substitutions, or insertions, suggest that students slow down to read accurately and to make it easier for listeners to understand them. Let's do a partner reading. Just for practice, I want you to slow down as much as you need to, to read every single word exactly the way it is written.
- Have students practice reading the text aloud with you or with another partner until they can read all words accurately. Remind them to self-correct as needed.

## Make It Harder

Students who are reading texts aloud with accuracy can continue their practice using longer or more challenging texts.

- Help pairs choose a text that interests them and that is at an appropriate level.
- Have partners take turns reading aloud to each other.
- Encourage partners to provide feedback to each other.

SIDE A
# Rate

FLUENCY
GRADE 3

**Rate** refers to oral reading at the speed of natural speech that demonstrates automatic word recognition and smooth pacing.

**Connect to *myView Literacy:***
**Fluency:** Unit 1, p. T56

## ROUTINE

### STEP 1 INTRODUCE

Describe the skill. Today we will practice reading aloud at an appropriate rate. A good rate is the speed we use when we talk with a friend. Reading aloud at an appropriate rate makes it easier for our listener to understand what we're reading.

### STEP 2 MODEL

- Display the beginning of a narrative text. As I read aloud, follow along and read silently with me. Notice the speed of my reading: I'm trying to read at a rate that's not too fast and not too slow. Model oral reading at an appropriate rate.
- The other thing I'm trying to do is keep an even pace throughout my reading. I don't want my reading to be too fast in some parts and too slow in others.

### STEP 3 GUIDE PRACTICE

- Distribute a copy of the same text to each student for choral reading. We'll read at the same speed that I just used. Read aloud the text with students.
- Lead students in reading aloud the same text again. Reading aloud at the right speed takes practice. Let's read aloud together once more.

### STEP 4 ON THEIR OWN

Have student pairs take turns continuing to read the story without you. When they have finished reading, make suggestions for speeding up or slowing down. For optimal fluency, have students read aloud the text three or four times.

# Rate



**CORRECTIVE FEEDBACK**

**IF** students are not reading aloud at an appropriate rate,

**THEN** model fluent oral reading with an appropriate rate, using Steps 2 and 3. Next, work through the Make It Easier activity.

## Make It Easier

Let students know whether they need to practice slowing down, speeding up, or maintaining an even pace. Then choose from the options below.

- Students who read slowly or with difficulty may benefit from a word-recognition activity. Make a set of word cards of the decodable words from the text and another set of high-frequency words. Use the cards as flashcards and have students first read aloud the decodable words until they read them at an appropriate rate. Guide students as needed. Repeat with high-frequency words.
- If students read too quickly, remind them that reading aloud is not a race and that it's important to understand the text as they read aloud. Try slowing down a bit. Sometimes if we read too quickly, we can miss a whole word or change the order of the words. Doing that could change the meaning of the text.
- If students read at an uneven pace, review punctuation cues and help them mark their copy of the text with slashes to indicate pauses. Let's read aloud together. We're going to read at a steady rate unless there's a reason to pause.
- Have partners read the text aloud until they read at an appropriate rate.

## Make It Harder

Encourage students who consistently read aloud at an appropriate rate to practice with longer or more challenging texts.

- Help students select a text at an appropriate level.
- Have partners take turns reading aloud. Have the listening partner provide feedback about how the reader's speed helped him or her understand the text.

**FLUENCY**
**GRADE 3**

**SIDE A**

# Prosody: Poetry

**Prosody** refers to oral reading with appropriate phrasing, intonation, and emphasis. **Rhythm** is the pattern of stressed and unstressed syllables. **Rhyme** is two or more words with the same middle and ending sounds.

**Connect to *myView Literacy:***
**Fluency:** Unit 3, p. T304

## ROUTINE

### STEP 1 INTRODUCE

Describe reading poetry aloud. Today we're going to practice reading poetry aloud. Poems often have rhythm, or a pattern of beats. Poems also often have rhyming words, such as *lunch* and *bunch,* which create patterns of sounds.

### STEP 2 MODEL

- Display a poem to model reading aloud. When I read a poem aloud, I read all the words the way they are written, the same as when I read other texts. Of course, I'll pause if I see a comma or a period. Indicate the stanzas, if applicable. I also pause when I see the space between the stanzas. Read the poem aloud.
- With poetry, my voice will show the sound devices, such as rhythm and rhyme, in the poem. Identify examples of words that rhyme in the poem. Words that rhyme, such as ____ and ____, create repeating sounds. I'm going to read aloud again and this time I'll tap the rhythm as I read.

### STEP 3 GUIDE PRACTICE

- Give a copy of the poem to each student. Let's read aloud together. Tap on your leg as you find the rhythm in the poem. Do a choral reading.
- Address prosody by asking students questions such as these: With a long word such as _____, which syllable is stressed? What other words or syllables do we emphasize, or stress, in this poem? How do the words themselves create the rhythm? What is an example of the rhythm? Do our voices go up or down on any words? Why? (Point out any question marks or exclamation points.) Read the poem aloud once more in a choral read.

### STEP 4 ON THEIR OWN

Have student pairs take turns reading the poem to each other. Provide feedback on students' volume and intonation. Encourage them to let the rhythm and rhyme guide their reading.

**SIDE B**

# Prosody: Poetry

**FLUENCY**
**GRADE 3**

### CORRECTIVE FEEDBACK

| | |
|---|---|
| **IF** students have difficulty reading a poem with prosody and recognizing rhythm and rhyme, | **THEN** model reading, using Steps 2 and 3. Next, work through the Make It Easier activity. |

## Make It Easier

If students are reading poetry without prosody, ensure they can read and understand all the words in the poem. Then choose from the options below.

- To help with their oral reading, students may benefit from discussing the meaning of the poem. What is the poem about? Is it about something you have experienced, or not? Is it a serious poem or a fun poem?
- Focus on rhythm and rhyme and discuss how those elements are important to the poem you are reading today. If a word is one syllable, it may or may not be stressed in a poem. It depends on the longer words around it. Have students underline multisyllabic words and circle the stressed syllable. The stresses in the longer words help set up the rhythm in the poem. Have students use a highlighter and indicate words that rhyme, or that have the same middle and ending sounds.
- Let's keep practicing until we can read the poem fluently. Read the poem aloud with students. Provide additional opportunities for students to practice reading aloud, either with a classmate or using a recording of the poem.

## Make It Harder

Have students who can read on-level poems with prosody read longer or more challenging poems.

- Help students select an appropriate poem and have them first read it silently. Encourage them to note rhyming words and to tap out the rhythm as they practice reading.
- Then have student pairs read aloud to each other and give each other feedback. Have them read aloud several times for optimal fluency practice.

SIDE A

# Prosody: Narrative Texts

**Prosody** refers to oral reading with appropriate phrasing, intonation, and emphasis. With **narrative texts,** reading aloud often involves reading with expression to help show characters' feelings.

**Connect to *myView Literacy:***
**Fluency:** Unit 1, p. T56

## ROUTINE

### STEP 1 INTRODUCE

Describe the skill. When we read narrative texts aloud, we speak loudly enough, and we read smoothly. We break longer sentences into meaningful phrases and use punctuation to guide our phrasing.

### STEP 2 MODEL

- Display a short narrative text with dialogue. I'm going to read smoothly and adjust my expression to show what is happening in the story. Model reading aloud the text.
- Use the following sentence frame with the Punctuation Cues to show how punctuation affects fluency. For example, say: When I see a _____, I know that my voice needs to _____. When I see quotation marks, I know that my voice needs to sound as a character would speak. Read the story again.

**Punctuation Cues for Fluency**

| | | |
|---|---|---|
| , | = | pause briefly |
| . | = | pause slightly longer |
| ? | = | raise voice |
| ! | = | show excitement |
| " " | = | read as the character would speak |

### STEP 3 GUIDE PRACTICE

- Give a copy of the story to each student. Let's read the first part together. Then stop to focus on intonation and emphasis. What is [character] feeling or thinking about? Which words from the text give you that information? How can we use our voices to show that feeling? Model an example from the text.
- Continue reading together. Note important punctuation and where students can read with expression to show how a character would speak.

### STEP 4 ON THEIR OWN

Have partners take turns reading the same text aloud with appropriate intonation, emphasis, and phrasing. Guide as needed.

SIDE B

# Prosody: Narrative Texts



**CORRECTIVE FEEDBACK**

| | |
|---|---|
| **IF** students have difficulty reading a narrative text with prosody, | **THEN** model reading with prosody, using Steps 2 and 3. Next, work through the Make It Easier activity. |

## Make It Easier

If students struggle to read with prosody, focus on the aspects that they find most challenging. Choose from the options below.

- Have students identify any words they are having difficulty with and work with them until they can read individual words fluently. Then do a partner reading.
- If students struggle with punctuation cues, review each symbol's meaning and how to pause or adjust their voices when reading. If students are reading word-by-word, help them chunk sentences into meaningful phrases on their copy. Have them practice reading the text aloud several times.
- If students have difficulty reading with expression, make sure they understand the text. For example, say, We know the character ____ is [excited/upset/wondering about something] here. How do you talk when you're feeling this way? Show that feeling when you're reading this part aloud.
- Do a partner reading with one student at a time. If students are reading too quietly, position yourself away from them and ask them to speak up, so you can hear them. Take turns reading parts of the story, and then repeat, switching roles.

## Make It Harder

Challenge students to be model readers for a partner or small group.

- Have the model reader first practice reading aloud with expression independently.
- Then have the reader lead a choral reading with a partner or small group.
- If recording devices are available, have students record themselves. Share readings with the class.

FLUENCY
GRADE 3

SIDE A

# Prosody: Informational Texts

**Prosody** refers to oral reading with appropriate phrasing, intonation, and emphasis.

**Connect to *myView Literacy:***
**Fluency:** Unit 1, p. T250

## ROUTINE

### STEP 1 INTRODUCE

Discuss prosody and informational texts. With informational texts, we pause when we see commas and periods. It's important to read with phrases, or groups of words. Phrases divide a sentence into parts, which help us understand meaning.

### STEP 2 MODEL

- Display a short informational text and read it aloud. Point out the phrasing. When I see commas or periods, I know to pause. I also pause before or after groups of words that go together, even if there's no comma. This shows the words go together.
- Explain intonation and emphasis. I use my voice to make my reading sound natural. To show emphasis, or get listeners' attention, I can slow down or change how loudly I'm speaking.

### STEP 3 GUIDE PRACTICE

- Distribute a copy of the text to each student. Let's do an echo reading. Read along and repeat after me, matching how I read.
- Ask students to reflect on intonation and emphasis. Did you hear my voice get louder or softer? Go up and down? What do you understand about the text when my voice changes?
- Start a discussion about phrasing. Let's look at the text together and identify where the pauses go. Guide students to notice the commas and periods. Where do you see a group of words that go together? Help students identify phrases.

### STEP 4 ON THEIR OWN

Have pairs take turns reading the text to each other with appropriate phrasing, intonation, and emphasis. Have partners provide feedback. For optimal fluency, have each student read aloud the text three times.

SIDE B

# Prosody: Informational Texts

**CORRECTIVE FEEDBACK**

**IF** students are not reading aloud with prosody,

**THEN** model how to read aloud with appropriate phrasing, intonation, and emphasis, using Steps 2 and 3. Next, work through the Make It Easier activity.

## Make It Easier

If students struggle to read with prosody, they may benefit from additional practice with phrasing.

- Have students practice reading aloud using a copy of the text in which pauses for phrasing are marked in the first paragraph or two. I put slashes between words to show the pauses. Read the paragraph aloud to model how the slashes work with the phrasing.
- Have students read the next paragraph silently. Then have students mark the paragraph with slashes to indicate pauses. Guide students as needed. When you're ready, read the paragraph aloud. Pause when you see a slash.
- Have students read aloud the text until they read with prosody.

## Make It Harder

You may want to have students who are fluent readers and who read aloud with appropriate phrasing be model readers.

- Give the student another informational text at the same level.
- Have the student practice reading the text aloud before modeling it with a partner, small group, or the whole class.
- Have the partners, small group, or class read aloud the text together twice more.

SIDE A

# Prosody: Drama

FLUENCY
GRADE 3

**Connect to *myView Literacy:***
**Fluency:** Unit 4, p. T302

**Prosody** refers to oral reading with appropriate phrasing, intonation, and emphasis. Oral reading of plays includes reading characters' dialogue with expression.

## ROUTINE

### STEP 1 INTRODUCE

Describe the skill. When we read drama aloud, we read the cast of characters, the setting, stage directions, and act and scene names in a neutral voice. We read dialogue with expression, and we let the punctuation guide us to read smoothly.

### STEP 2 MODEL

- Display the first part of a drama. Model reading it aloud, including all the text. Remind students to read dialogue with expression and text such as stage directions in a neutral voice.
- The punctuation helps me know if the character is asking a question or is excited. Stage directions instruct the actor how to deliver the lines, so they tell me, too, how to read the dialogue. Model reading aloud again, with expression, to show character.

Punctuation Cues for Fluency

, = pause briefly

. = pause slightly longer

? = raise voice

! = show excitement

" " = read as the character would speak

### STEP 3 GUIDE PRACTICE

- Give each student a copy of the play. Let's read aloud from the beginning together.
- Ask questions to draw students' attention to volume, expression, phrasing, and punctuation. How does reading aloud with expression help us understand and enjoy the play? Why is it important to read some parts in a neutral voice? Read aloud the first part together again.

### STEP 4 ON THEIR OWN

Assign roles to student pairs. Have partners continue reading the play aloud. Provide feedback about phrasing, intonation, emphasis, and expression.

SIDE B

# Prosody: Drama

## CORRECTIVE FEEDBACK

**IF** students have difficulty reading a dramatic text with prosody,

**THEN** model reading with prosody, using Steps 2 and 3. Next, work through the Make It Easier activity.

## Make It Easier

Students who struggle with reading with prosody in drama may need help with particular aspects, such as phrasing or expression. Choose from the options below.

- Ask students to give a brief summary of the text to ensure they understand it.
- If students ignore punctuation cues, review what the symbols mean and how they help readers know where to pause and adjust their voices. You may want to use a recording of the text to provide additional models of fluent oral reading.
- Discuss each character, how he or she could be portrayed, and demonstrate how you can adjust your voice to show the character's thoughts and feelings. Have students focus on the lines of dialogue for one character at a time.
- Now let's practice reading the text several times. Once individual students are reading with some fluency, have them practice with partners.

## Make It Harder

Have students who can read on-level dramatic texts with prosody perform a Readers' Theater.

- Help students choose an appropriate play, and provide each student with a copy. Model reading the play aloud with prosody.
- Choose students to read the various parts including a narrator, if necessary. Allow students time to practice reading their character's lines with expression.
- Have students perform the Readers' Theater for the class.

# Fluency and Qualitative Measures

### What Is Fluency?

Fluency is reading accurately, with expression, at an appropriate rate. To learn to read words and become fluent readers, students need a solid phonological base and strong alphabetic and language skills. Frequent practice reading high-frequency words helps students learn to recognize words automatically.

As students' ability to read words with automaticity grows, they begin to understand the text as they read and will be able to demonstrate different aspects of prosody as they read aloud. Fluent readers group words into meaningful phrases and use their voices to convey the meaning of a text by adjusting timing, expression, volume, emphasis, and intonation. As students make gains in fluency, they will read more quickly while maintaining accuracy and demonstrating expression.

Fluency is directly related to comprehending text, the ultimate goal of reading. Mastery of these skills—reading accurately with automaticity, at an appropriate rate, and with appropriate expression—is what helps students focus on the meaning of a text.

### What Does a Fluency Test Measure?

A fluency test measures the number of words that a student reads aloud correctly in one minute (WCPM) in a grade-level text that the student has not previously seen. Speed, while an important indicator, is not the main objective.

- **Accuracy, Rate, and WCPM** The score (words correctly read per minute) is calculated by subtracting the number of errors the student makes from the total number of words the student read.
- **Results** Scores can be highly variable because of familiarity (or lack of familiarity) with a particular topic and related vocabulary, or due to student anxiety. The score of any one test should be seen within the context of a semester or a year.

### Using *myView Cold Reads for Fluency and Comprehension*

*Cold Reads for Fluency and Comprehension* provides leveled selections and comprehension items that assess each week's comprehension focus and support emerging fluency.

- **Differentiation** Selections and items are written for students at varying levels of proficiency, as indicated at the bottom of each page: Developing (D), On-Level (OL), and Advanced (A).
- **High-Frequency Words** High-frequency words are strategically placed in the selections to give students additional practice reading these words in context.
- **Practice** Use selections to model fluent oral reading regularly in class. Have students practice reading selections orally to prepare for assessment.
- **Assessment** Selections are designed to be administered as tests to assess student progress.

### Qualitative Measures

Gaining fluency is a process that is different for every reader. Some students demonstrate fluency from early on, while for others it can be a gradual process. Over time and with effective reading instruction and practice, students will show improvement. Charting WCPM scores as students' reading improves motivates them to further practice and improve their fluency.

### Key Variables

Emerging readers progress through phases, the timing of which varies but can be generalized as follows:

- A focus on pronouncing words and phrases (Kindergarten, Grade 1, and first half of Grade 2)
- Showing signs of prosody; starting to use expressive language (second half of Grade 2)
- Fluctuating oral reading fluency scores (at the end of Grade 3, moving into Grades 4 and 5)

### Measuring Other Aspects of Fluency

To get an overall picture of a student's fluency, teachers will benefit from tracking not only WCPM but also those elements of prosody that are more subjective. As you listen to students' oral reading practice, pay attention to their demonstration of prosodic elements beyond accuracy and rate.

- **Phrasing** Does the student group words into meaningful chunks and pause appropriately when encountering commas and periods?
- **Intonation** Does the student's voice go up and down when she or he sees a question mark or exclamation mark, or when speaking as a character would?
- **Volume and Stress** Does the student translate the emotion and meaning of the text into his or her oral reading through appropriate shifts in volume and emphasis?
- **Self-correction** Does the student self-correct, an important fluency and comprehension skill, as he or she reads?

Use the **Oral Reading Fluency Rubric** to determine a student's level of fluency and assess areas in which a student may need practice.

# Target Fluency Goals

One of the most effective ways to assess fluency is by taking a timed sample of a student's oral reading and measuring words correct per minute (WCPM).

**Prepare for the Timed Sample**

- Choose a selection that is on grade level and not previously seen by the student.
- Make two copies of the selection. Give one copy to the student and keep the other copy for yourself.
- Have a timer or clock available for timing the reading.

**Administer the Timed Sample**

- Have the student read aloud the selection for one minute, excluding the title.
- Mark on your copy of the selection any errors the student makes.
- Stop the student at exactly one minute and note precisely where he or she stopped.

**Score the Results:** WCPM = (Total number of words read) – (Number of errors)

- Count the total number of words read in one minute.
- Subtract the number of errors made.
- Record the words correct per minute score.

**Interpret the Score**

The following chart identifies performance benchmarks for fall, winter, and spring, with the expected benchmark at the 50th percentile. For example, a third-grade student reading 137 WCPM in winter is reading at the 75th percentile. The same student reading 166 WCPM in the spring is now reading at the 90th percentile.

| GRADE | %ILE | FALL WCPM | WINTER WCPM | SPRING WCPM |
|---|---|---|---|---|
| 3 | 90 | 134 | 161 | 166 |
| | 75 | 104 | 137 | 139 |
| | 50 | 83 | 97 | 112 |
| | 25 | 59 | 79 | 91 |
| | 20 | 40 | 62 | 63 |

Hasbrouck, J. & Tindal, G. (2017). "Compiled ORF Norms 2017" from *An Update to Compiled ORF Norms (Technical Report No. 1702)*. Eugene, OR, Behavioral Research and Teaching, University of Oregon. Used by permission.

**IF** the score is lower than the expected benchmark,

**THEN** evaluate your notes on the student's errors to determine whether further instruction in decoding, vocabulary, and comprehension strategies is needed. Exposing the student to fluent reading models and encouraging the student to read more texts at an accessible reading level may also increase fluency.

# Oral Reading Fluency Rubric

| Score | VOLUME AND EXPRESSION | SYNTAX AND PHRASING | ACCURACY | RATE |
|---|---|---|---|---|
| 4 | The student reads enthusiastically with good expression throughout the text and varies expression and volume to match his or her interpretation of the text. | The student reads smoothly with some breaks; demonstrates meaningful phrasing, mostly in clause and sentence units; adjusts for punctuation; and preserves the author's syntax. Stress and intonation are appropriate. | The student reads accurately. A rare, minor error may occur or be self-corrected, but does not appear to detract from the overall comprehension of the text. | The student consistently reads at a natural-sounding, conversational pace. |
| 3 | The student reads with appropriate volume and some expression appropriate to the text. | The student generally uses appropriate phrasing but occasionally breaks smoothness with run-ons or mid-sentence pauses for breath, or does not adjust for punctuation. Stress and intonation are adequate, and the syntax of the author is mostly preserved. | The student mostly reads accurately. Errors sometimes result from a difficult word or sentence structure. Errors may be self-corrected and do not appear to affect comprehension. | The student sometimes reads at an uneven pace, too slow or too fast at times. |
| 2 | The student begins to use voice to make text sound natural but focuses mostly on reading the words and reads somewhat quietly. Expression is minimal. | The student reads in short phrases and does not adjust for punctuation, making the reading sound choppy. Stress and intonation are lacking or inappropriate at times. | The student makes a number of errors. Errors sometimes affect comprehension. | The student reads somewhat slowly. There may be frequent or extended pauses or hesitations. |
| 1 | The student reads the words but does not sound natural, is difficult to hear, and uses little or no expression. | The student reads in a choppy, word-by-word manner with frequent extended pauses, hesitations, false starts, sound-outs, repetitions, and/or multiple attempts. Stress and intonation are absent or inappropriate. | The student makes many errors to the point of affecting comprehension. | The student reads slowly and with difficulty. |

# Self-Monitor Fluency

*Self-monitoring in reading means being aware when you successfully construct the author's message and when you notice something is amiss with meaning, structure, or graphophonic information. . . . Self-monitoring and self-correction appear frequently in research records of young readers making strong progress and less frequently for those making slow progress.*

—Nancy L. Anderson, Elizabeth L. Kaye

"Finding Versus Fixing: Self-Monitoring for Readers Who Struggle"

*The Reading Teacher*, Vol. 70, No. 5, March/April 2017

FLUENCY
GRADE 3

SIDE A

# Self-Monitor: Oral Reading

When readers **self-monitor** oral reading, they listen as they read to notice and correct word-reading errors and to confirm understanding.

## ROUTINE

### STEP 1 INTRODUCE

As we read aloud today, we're going to think about our reading. We'll pay attention to whether the words sound right and make sense. If we notice something isn't quite right, we'll pause and use fix-up strategies. Review the strategies with students.

### STEP 2 MODEL

Display the text and tell students you are going to read aloud. I'm going to read all the words as they are written. I won't skip, add, or change words. I'll read at an appropriate rate and I'll pay attention to punctuation. As I read, I'll ask myself: Does this make sense? If it doesn't, I'll pause and use the fix-up strategies. When I see new words in the text, I'll use my word-reading skills to read them.

**Lakes and ponds have many tiny plants and animals living in them. They are very small, but you can see them with a magnifying glass or a special tool called a microscope. These microscopic plants and animals are food for each other. The way that these plants and animals eat and are eaten is so complicated that we call it a food web.**

Fix-Up Strategies

- If it doesn't make sense, pause.
- Think about what is confusing.
- For tricky words, look for word parts or vowel patterns you know. Look at word endings.
- Reread.
- Ask for help.

As you read, substitute the word *microscope* for *microscopic* and model using the strategies. I'm going to pause because that sentence didn't sound right. I read the word *microscope,* but now I see that this word has the ending *-ic.* The ending changes how I say the base word: *microscope, microscopic.* I'll reread the sentence to see if *microscopic* makes sense.

### STEP 3 GUIDE PRACTICE

Display the same text for choral reading. Let's read aloud together. We'll read accurately and smoothly at the rate that I just used.

### STEP 4 ON THEIR OWN

Help students choose an appropriate text and have pairs take turns reading aloud. As you read, listen to yourself to check if your reading makes sense. Pause if you notice that something isn't quite right. Use the fix-up strategies to help you.

**SIDE B**

# Self-Monitor: Oral Reading

**CORRECTIVE FEEDBACK**

| | |
|---|---|
| **IF** students are not self-monitoring their reading, | **THEN** model self-monitoring, using Steps 2 and 3. Next, work through the Make It Easier activity. |

## Make It Easier

Watch for and encourage self-monitoring behaviors.

- Remind students that you want them to think about their reading. As you read, I want you to pay close attention to make sure your reading makes sense. Noticing errors and fixing them will help you better understand what you read.
- Display an appropriate text and ask students to read aloud. Observe students for self-monitoring behaviors, such as making a comment or attempting to self-correct. Ask: What made you stop? What did you notice?
- If a student makes an error that affects meaning but does not notice, wait until they get to the end of the sentence or the paragraph. Ask: Will you reread that? Help students decode tricky words. Then, have them reread to check whether the word makes sense in the sentence and with the rest of the text.

## Make It Harder

Students who self-monitor and self-correct as they read can continue practicing using longer or more challenging texts.

- Help students choose an appropriate text.
- Ask partners to take turns reading aloud to each other. Encourage students to read with accuracy and at a good rate, and to pay attention to punctuation. Remind them to notice whether the text makes sense and to pause and use the strategies when needed.

SIDE A

# Self-Monitor: Silent Reading

When readers **self-monitor** silent reading, they pay attention to their reading to make sure they read fluently, maintain focus, and understand what they read.

## ROUTINE

### STEP 1 INTRODUCE

Today we're going to practice silent reading. As we read, we're going to pay close attention to our reading. If we notice that we don't understand something, get stuck on a tricky word, or lose our focus, we'll pause and reread. Review the fix-up strategies with students.

### STEP 2 MODEL

- Display a short text and model your thinking. As I read, I'm going to listen to my inner voice. I'm going to keep checking in with myself and thinking about what I'm reading. I'll ask myself: Does this make sense? If it doesn't, I'll pause and use the fix-up strategies.
- If a word or sentence I read doesn't sound right or make sense, I'm going to pause and reread. For tricky words, I'll use a word-reading strategy, such as looking for word parts or vowel patterns I know. Then I'll go back to the beginning of the sentence and reread to make sure the word makes sense in the sentence and with the rest of the text.

Fix-Up Strategies

- If you've lost focus or it doesn't make sense, pause.
- Reread.
- For tricky words, look for word parts or vowel patterns you know.
- Make a note or ask for help.

### STEP 3 GUIDE PRACTICE

Have students read the same text silently. Remind them to pay attention to their reading and pause to use fix-up strategies when needed. When students are finished, ask volunteers to share the strategies they used. Then, discuss the text as a group. Ask students questions, such as which part of the text helped them picture the setting.

### STEP 4 ON THEIR OWN

Help each student choose an appropriate text for silent reading. As you read, remember to pay close attention to your reading and listen to your inner voice. Make sure you read the words correctly and you understand what you read. Pause to use the fix-up strategies when you need to. When students are finished, ask volunteers to share a strategy they used. Then, have them share with a partner the most interesting thing they read.

SIDE B

# Self-Monitor: Silent Reading

**CORRECTIVE FEEDBACK**

| | |
|---|---|
| **IF** students are not self-monitoring their reading, | **THEN** model thinking about self-monitoring during silent reading, using Steps 2 and 3. Next, work through the Make It Easier activity. |

## Make It Easier

Guide students to self-monitor as they read silently.

- Remind students that you want them to think about their reading as they read silently. As you read, I want you to pay close attention to your reading and listen to your inner voice. If something doesn't make sense, pause and go back to reread.
- Have students read a section of text silently, then have them stop and answer a question you ask about the text. If students have trouble answering the question, help them use the strategies and focus on what they need to reread.

## Make It Harder

Students who are self-monitoring as they read silently can continue practicing using longer or more challenging texts.

- Help students choose a text at an appropriate level and ask them to read silently.
- When students finish reading, ask them to tell a partner about what they read or write one thing the author wanted them to know.

# Comprehension

*Because motivation is inherently social, the social context of the classroom can be adapted and leveraged to better support reading motivation* (Hruby et al., 2016). *In fact, a recent systematic review and meta-analysis found that motivational reading interventions, such as fostering reading interest through hands-on activities, offering choices, and providing process-oriented feedback, produced significant, positive effects on students' reading motivations and reading comprehension* (McBreen & Savage, 2020).

—Nell K. Duke, Alessandra E. Ward, P. David Pearson

"The Science of Reading Comprehension Instruction"

*The Reading Teacher*, Vol. 74, No. 6, May/June 2021

## COMPREHENSION
GRADE 3

SIDE A

# Build Background Knowledge

Readers **build background knowledge** to connect their own background to a text to better understand it, and then add more knowledge from the text as they read.

**Connect to *myView Literacy:***
**Introduce the Text:** Unit 1, p. T28

# ROUTINE

## STEP 1 INTRODUCE

When we read, we connect what we know to the text. Making connections to our own experiences, other texts, and the world helps us understand what we're reading.

## STEP 2 MODEL

- Display a short, familiar text. Before we read, we preview the text. We think about what we already know about the topic or story. Walk through a preview of the first part of the text. Discuss what you learn from the preview and model making connections.
- As I read, I pause. I think more about what I know about texts like this. *How is this like similar texts I have read?* Demonstrate using questions such as the ones at the right to help students make connections and build background knowledge.
- At the end of a section or the whole text, I ask if I've learned something new about the world that I didn't know before.

## STEP 3 GUIDE PRACTICE

Guide students to use their background knowledge to make connections about another section of the text. Guide a preview. Ask students to tell what they already know about similar texts they have read. As students read, have them pause to make connections.

## STEP 4 ON THEIR OWN

Have students read an unfamiliar text of the same genre. Ask them to share how they use their background knowledge to connect with and understand the text.

For literary texts, I ask:

- Have I ever met someone like this character?
- Have I ever felt the way this character feels?
- Have I read other stories like this?
- What type of message do those stories convey?

For informational texts, I ask:

- What do I know about this topic?
- What information have I learned from texts like this one?
- How are details from this time period similar to events today?
- What new ideas about my own world am I learning?

SIDE B

# Build Background Knowledge

**CORRECTIVE FEEDBACK**

| | |
|---|---|
| **IF** students cannot build background knowledge for a text, | **THEN** model how to build background knowledge, using Steps 2 and 3. Next, work through the Make It Easier activity. |

## Make It Easier

Some students may struggle to use background knowledge to make connections between texts. Use two or more short texts of a similar genre, such as two of Aesop's fables, and walk students through making connections.

- Preview and read aloud one text. Discuss the story's main characters, events, and lesson, or moral.
- Now let's read another [genre of the text]. We have just read a text very similar to it. So before we read, we can think about that other text. What do we know about texts like this? Discuss elements, such as types of characters, setting, and the lesson, or moral.
- Read and discuss the text, guiding students to make connections as you read. As time permits, continue with additional texts in the genre.

## Make It Harder

Students may benefit from making connections between texts by the same author, such as books in a series.

- Ask students to name a text by a familiar author. Then have students choose an unfamiliar book by the same author.
- Have partners preview the text and list what they already know about it, focusing on what they know about the author's other texts.
- Have partners read the text, making connections as they read.
- Have partners explain how this author's work connects to what they know about the real world. What do these texts have to say about the world in general?

**SIDE A**

# Ask and Answer Questions

**COMPREHENSION**
GRADE 3

Readers **ask and answer questions** about the text before, during, and after reading to deepen understanding and gain information.

**Connect to *myView Literacy:***
**Ask and Answer Questions:** Unit 1, p. T128

# ROUTINE

## STEP 1 INTRODUCE

When we read, we ask ourselves questions about the ideas and concepts in a text before, during, and after we read. Asking questions and looking for answers in the text gives us a reason to read. Asking questions also helps us better understand the text.

## STEP 2 MODEL

- Display a familiar text. Before I read, I look at the cover, title, illustrations, and any text features. I ask myself questions based on this preview. Preview the text and write questions.
- As I read, I'll look for answers to my first questions. I also ask questions about things in the text I don't understand. Begin reading aloud a section of the text. Pause to note details that answer your initial questions or new parts in the text that may be confusing. I can reread to see if that helps answer my questions.
- After finishing a section, review your questions and answers so far. After reading, I think about the answers I found. I may have more questions, such as why the author wrote this text or what the theme is. I can reread or read on to answer these questions.

## STEP 3 GUIDE PRACTICE

Guide students to generate and answer questions about the rest of the text. After reading, discuss students' answers. Discuss how the questions helped them think about the author's purpose and key ideas.

## STEP 4 ON THEIR OWN

Have students read a brief unfamiliar text. Ask them to list their questions and answers before, during, and after reading. Then have students use their answers to discuss the text's key ideas or theme.

Before Reading
- What is the story about?
- Who are the characters and where are they?
- What will the text tell about the topic?
- Why did the author write this text?

During Reading
- Why are the characters acting this way?
- What new information am I learning?

After Reading
- Why did the story end this way?
- What are the key ideas?
- What lesson or message does the author want me to learn?

SIDE B

# Ask and Answer Questions

### CORRECTIVE FEEDBACK

**IF** students cannot ask and answer questions about a text,

**THEN** model how to ask and answer questions, using Steps 2 and 3. Next, work through the Make It Easier activity.

## Make It Easier

Some students may have trouble generating high-level questions. Use an unfamiliar text with illustrations to guide students to ask and adjust questions.

- Preview the text. Ask: What might this story be about? What might you want to learn about this topic or these characters? Write students' questions. Adjust the questions so that they are more focused on key plot elements or ideas. For example, for *James and the Giant Peach,* instead of *Who is James?* you might ask *What is James going to do with a giant peach?* Avoid yes/no questions.
- Continue previewing the illustrations. Write down students' questions for each illustration, adjusting the wording as needed.
- When you finish the preview, review the questions. Discuss which ones seem to be most important to answer to understand the text. Point out that when students read the text, they will look for details that answer these questions.

## Make It Harder

Students who can ask and answer questions may benefit from working with a partner to ask and answer Five *W*s and *H* questions about an unfamiliar text.

- Review questions that begin with *Who, What, When, Where, Why,* and *How.* Model examples of each type.
- Have partners choose, preview, and read together an unfamiliar text. Challenge students to write at least one question for each of the Five *W*s and *H* questions before, during, and after they read. Remind them to write high-level questions that require deep thinking about the text. As partners read, they should look for the answers.
- When partners are done reading and have answered their questions, discuss which questions best helped them understand the deeper meaning of the text.

**COMPREHENSION**
GRADE 3

**SIDE A**

# Predictions

To make **predictions** means to tell what a text might be about or what might happen next in the text, based on details in the text.

**Connect to *myView Literacy:***
**Correct or Confirm Predictions:**
Unit 3, p. T66

# ROUTINE

## STEP 1 INTRODUCE

To make predictions, we use clues in the text, images, text features, and text structure to tell what a text will be about or what we think will happen. This helps us read for a purpose. We adjust predictions as we read.

## STEP 2 MODEL

- Choose an unfamiliar text. I start by previewing. Use the questions at the right to model making predictions. Explain how you can use what you know about the genre to predict. For a story, you might make predictions about setting and events. Make a prediction using the frame: Based on [detail], I predict _____.
- Now I read to confirm, or check, my predictions. Read aloud a section. Use the second set of questions at the right as a guide. I predicted _____. I know my prediction is [correct/incorrect] because _____. Point out specific details in the text as support.
- If my prediction is correct, I can confirm it with text details. If it is incorrect, I use text details to correct it. I also think about what I've read so far to make new predictions. Write a new prediction.

Make Predictions

- What do text features such as title, headings, and images show?
- What do I already know about this type of text?
- What do I think will happen? What will I learn about? Why?

Confirm or Correct Predictions

- Were my predictions correct? What details in the text confirm them?
- If my predictions are incorrect, how should I correct them?
- What can I predict now? Why?

## STEP 3 GUIDE PRACTICE

Use the questions to guide students to make predictions about a short illustrated story. After reading, have students explain their predictions—whether they were correct, how they know, and how they corrected them.

## STEP 4 ON THEIR OWN

Have students write a set of predictions before and while they read a new text independently. Then discuss how they confirmed or corrected their predictions after reading. Guide students as needed.

# Predictions



## CORRECTIVE FEEDBACK

**IF** students cannot predict what will happen as they read,

**THEN** model how to make and confirm or correct predictions with an easier, illustrated text, using Steps 2 and 3. Next, work through the Make It Easier activity.

## Make It Easier

Students who struggle with predicting may benefit from practice using genre knowledge to make predictions.

- Display a short fairy tale with illustrations, ideally one students have not read. Ask students to name other fairy tales they know. Review the list of questions at the right. Discuss students' answers. You can use what you know about the genre to help make predictions.
- Preview the illustrations. Ask: What is the setting? What events might happen in a setting like this? Record and discuss predictions. Continue to make predictions about the characters, events, and ending.
- Read aloud the text. As you read, guide students to confirm or correct predictions. Have them make new predictions using what they know about the genre.

What I Know About Fairy Tales

- What happens in fairy tales?
- What settings and types of characters do fairy tales have?
- What problems do characters solve?
- How do fairy tales often end?

## Make It Harder

Extend the activity by having students make predictions about a text in a different genre. Provide students with a text in a familiar genre, such as historical fiction.

- Have partners list the types of settings, characters, events, and endings that often occur in the genre. Ask: What do you already know about texts like this?
- Have partners preview the text and write predictions. Then have them read the text together to confirm or correct their predictions.
- When partners are finished reading, have them take turns explaining how they used what they know about the genre to make predictions and how they were able to confirm or correct their predictions.

**SIDE A**

# Make Inferences

**COMPREHENSION**
GRADE 3

**Connect to *myView Literacy:***
**Infer Theme:** Unit 1, p. T120

To make **inferences,** readers combine what they know with details they read to understand ideas that are not directly stated in the text.

## ROUTINE

### STEP 1 INTRODUCE

Authors do not state every idea directly in the text. Readers can discover these ideas by making inferences, or good guesses. To do this, we combine details from the text with what we already know.

### STEP 2 MODEL

- Read aloud a story that students are familiar with, such as "Stone Soup." Authors often don't tell readers exactly what the lesson or theme in a story is. But I can make inferences about the lesson or theme.
- Model using text details as clues. The author doesn't say what lesson the townspeople learn. But we can use clues in the text to figure that out. The townspeople end up sharing food with the traveler, and he shares his soup.
- Model using prior knowledge. I know that sharing with others often makes people happy.
- Make an inference. I combine the text evidence with what I already know about sharing. I make an inference about a lesson in the story: *When people share, everyone is happier.* Making inferences helps me understand this theme.

To make inferences, I . . .

- look for details, or clues, in the text.
- think about what I already know that relates to the text.
- combine what I read and what I know to better understand the characters, events, themes, or ideas in the text.

### STEP 3 GUIDE PRACTICE

Use the steps in the right column above. Guide students to make another inference about being kind to others in "Stone Soup."

### STEP 4 ON THEIR OWN

Have students choose another familiar story. Have them follow the steps independently to make an inference about the characters, events, and theme. Guide students as needed.

SIDE B

# Make Inferences

### CORRECTIVE FEEDBACK

**IF** students cannot make inferences as they read,

**THEN** model how to use text details and prior knowledge to make inferences, using Steps 2 and 3. Next, work through the Make It Easier activity.

## Make It Easier

Students may benefit from practicing with an Aesop's fable such as "The Ant and the Grasshopper."

- Display a short version of the fable. Read aloud the text, leaving out the moral at the end.
- Create a three-column chart with the following heads: *Text Details, What I Know,* and *Inference: Life Lesson.* Fill it in as you make an inference.
- First, we list text details. What do the ant and the grasshopper do? (The ant works hard to prepare for winter, but the grasshopper does not prepare.) What usually happens when people are not prepared? (They may have a hard time.) What happens at the end of the story? (The grasshopper is not ready for winter and is unhappy.)
- We combine text details with what we know to make an inference about the lesson: *Always be prepared.*

Text Details
- What the ant does
- What the grasshopper does

What I Know
- What I know about being prepared

Inference: Life Lesson

## Make It Harder

Students can extend the activity by identifying and comparing similar themes in folktales.

- Give student pairs two folktales with similar themes. Have partners work together to use text details and what they know about life to infer at least one main theme in each story.
- Have them fill out a three-column chart similar to the one in Make It Easier for each story.
- Have students explain how they used the text details and prior knowledge to infer each theme. Then have them compare themes.

**COMPREHENSION**
GRADE 3

SIDE A

# Main Idea and Details

**Main ideas** are the most important ideas, or big ideas. **Details** are smaller, often interesting pieces of information that tell more about the main ideas.

**Connect to *myView Literacy:***
**Identify Main Idea and Details:**
Unit 2, p. T50

## ROUTINE

### STEP 1 INTRODUCE

The main ideas are the most important ideas about the topic in a text. Details give more information about the main ideas. The most important details help us figure out the main ideas.

### STEP 2 MODEL

- Display an informational text. First, I identify the topic. I look at the title, sentences, and images and ask, *What or who is the text mostly about?* Point out related words and repeated ideas in the text or images. Then state the topic.
- As I read, I ask, *What is the most important idea about the topic?* Walk through each sentence. Model sorting important details from interesting but unimportant details. The important details, or key details, are clues to the main idea(s). Details may lead to more than one main idea.
- I look at the key details to figure out the main ideas in the text. State a main idea and explain how the details helped you identify it. Continue reading, using key details to help identify additional main ideas.

### STEP 3 GUIDE PRACTICE

Display an informational text. Have students use the questions at the right to identify main idea(s). How do details support the main idea(s)?

### STEP 4 ON THEIR OWN

Have students choose a familiar informational text. Have them write at least one main idea and list the key details. Ask them to explain how the details support the main idea. Guide as needed.

**To Find the Main Idea**

- **Identify the Topic**
  Who or what is the text mostly about?
- **Look at the Details**
  What are the key details? Which details tell about the most important ideas?
- **Figure Out the Main Ideas**
  What are the most important ideas about the topic that the author wants me to know?

**COMPREHENSION**
**GRADE 3**

**SIDE B**

# Main Idea and Details

**CORRECTIVE FEEDBACK**

**IF** students cannot identify an implied main idea in a text,

**THEN** model the process again, using Steps 2 and 3. Next, work through the Make It Easier activity.

## Make It Easier

Students may benefit from distinguishing stated and implied main ideas.

- Display the text at the right. Sometimes authors directly state a main idea in the text. Read aloud the first paragraph. The first sentence tells a main idea about dogs: "All dogs have certain common characteristics." The rest of the sentences give details that tell more about this idea.
- Often authors do not say the main idea directly. We need to look at the details for clues. Read aloud the second paragraph. Each sentence gives a detail about dogs. What idea do all these details support?
- List three possible main ideas: *1. Dogs are great hunters. 2. Dogs are kind to people. 3. Dogs make great pets.* Guide students to see that the details all support choice 3. When the main idea isn't stated, we identify it and state it in our own words: *Dogs make great pets.*

All dogs have certain common characteristics. They are mammals that walk on their toes. They have body hair called fur. They have teeth that are good for eating meat.

Dogs are loyal to humans. They can be friendly and loving. Dogs often protect human friends and help with tasks such as hunting or herding sheep.

## Make It Harder

Students can extend the activity by identifying the main idea of a whole text.

- Provide students with a brief informational text. In addition to main ideas in paragraphs, a longer text usually has a main idea—the most important idea of the whole text.
- Have students read the text and identify the main ideas throughout the text.
- Then have students write a main idea for the whole text, explaining how the details and other main ideas support it.

**COMPREHENSION**
GRADE 3

SIDE A

# Monitor Comprehension

To **monitor comprehension,** readers use different strategies to make sure they comprehend what they are reading.

**Connect to *myView Literacy:***
**Monitor Comprehension:** Unit 2, p. T58

## ROUTINE

### STEP 1 INTRODUCE

As we read, we monitor comprehension, or check our understanding. If our understanding breaks down, we try different strategies, or tools, to clarify anything in the text that doesn't make sense.

### STEP 2 MODEL

- Read aloud a section or paragraph of a text. As I read, I stop to make sure the text makes sense. If it's clear, I keep reading.
- Sometimes I find a word or idea that I don't understand. I stop, make a note, and then use one or more strategies to help me understand. Point out a confusing word or section in the text. Note your confusion. Then review the strategies at the right. Model using the appropriate strategy to clear up your confusion.
- Continue reading, modeling how to apply different strategies to resolve other points of confusion. Point out that different strategies are more helpful for different sticking points, and that the goal is to use them as needed so that the entire text makes sense.

Monitor Comprehension "Fix-Up" Strategies

- Reread to look for details I may have missed.
- Think about what I already know.
- Look at text features for important details.
- Check a resource such as a dictionary.
- Ask for help.

### STEP 3 GUIDE PRACTICE

Guide students to apply relevant strategies to another part of the text. Ask them to identify a confusing part and pick a strategy to help monitor their comprehension. Have students explain why they chose the strategy they did and how they used it to clear up confusion.

### STEP 4 ON THEIR OWN

Have students read a new text. Have them pause to monitor comprehension and apply the strategies. Guide students as needed.

SIDE B

# Monitor Comprehension

### CORRECTIVE FEEDBACK

**IF** students cannot apply strategies to monitor comprehension as they read,

**THEN** model how to apply different strategies for different purposes, using Steps 2 and 3. Next, work through the Make It Easier activity.

## Make It Easier

Students who struggle to apply appropriate comprehension strategies may benefit from reviewing which strategies work best for different purposes.

- Choose a short text with images. Point out that when students don't understand a main idea in a text, rereading can help clarify the idea. I might need to reread a few sentences or a whole section. I look for supporting details that help me understand the idea. Model rereading to clarify a main idea.
- Explain that rereading can also help readers find context clues—such as synonyms, antonyms, or examples—to the meanings of unfamiliar words.
- Point out that analyzing images can also help clarify ideas or word meanings. Model using the images in the text to clarify a main idea or the meaning of an unfamiliar word.
- Finally, walk students through using a dictionary or asking for help. Explain that these strategies are useful if students still struggle after trying other strategies.

## Make It Harder

Students who can apply the strategies effectively can demonstrate how they monitor comprehension to a partner.

- Have partners take turns reading a text aloud to each other. As each partner reads, he or she should stop at different points to monitor comprehension using the following frames: *I understand ______. But I'm not sure about ______. So I will ______ to clarify my understanding.*
- The reader should note the confusion and pick a strategy. Then he or she should demonstrate using the strategy to clear up the confusion.
- After the partner has clarified understanding, he or she can summarize the section of text and explain why the strategy or strategies was helpful.

SIDE A

# Summarize

**COMPREHENSION**
GRADE 3

To **summarize** is to restate in your own words the most important ideas or events of a text in a shorter version of the original.

**Connect to *myView Literacy:***
**Summarize Informational Text:**
Unit 3, p. T248

## ROUTINE

### STEP 1 INTRODUCE

A summary shows my understanding of what I have read. To summarize a text, I find the most important ideas in the text. I use my own words to restate these ideas clearly.

### STEP 2 MODEL

- Display and read aloud a short, familiar informational text. To summarize a text, I read each paragraph to find out what it is about. This is the key idea of the paragraph. Point to and reread the text that presents the key idea. I say this key idea in my own words. Restate the idea.
- Then I look at sentences in the paragraph for the most important information about the key idea. Model sorting through the sentences. Demonstrate separating information that is important—or that helps readers understand the key idea—from information that may be interesting but is less important for understanding the key idea. I include only the most important information.
- Next I summarize the paragraph by using my own words to state the key idea and important information in one sentence.

### STEP 3 GUIDE PRACTICE

Review the steps at the right with students. Then guide them to summarize the next paragraph in the same text.

### STEP 4 ON THEIR OWN

Now have students follow the steps to summarize the next paragraph in the same text. Ask them to explain why they chose the ideas they did in their summaries. Guide students as needed.

To summarize, I...
- find the key idea of each paragraph.
- restate the key idea in my own words.
- find the most important information about the key idea.
- restate only the key idea and most important information in my own words.

**SIDE B**

# Summarize

**COMPREHENSION**
**GRADE 3**

**CORRECTIVE FEEDBACK**

**IF** students cannot summarize information in texts,

**THEN** model how to identify the key idea and important information, using Steps 2 and 3. Next, work through the Make It Easier activity.

## Make It Easier

Students who struggle with summarizing might need more support discerning important from unimportant information.

- Read aloud the entire text at the right. Then point to the first two sentences and identify the key idea of the text. (Cats knead with their paws for good reasons.)
- We'll look for the most important information about this key idea. Not all pieces of information may be important. Reread each sentence aloud. Have students give a thumbs up if a sentence is important and a thumbs down if it's not. Why is this information important or not important? (Sentence 3: Not important; it doesn't tell why cats knead with their paws. Sentences 4 and 5: Important; these are reasons why cats knead with their paws.)
- Work with students to summarize the text in their own words.

Cats sometimes look like they are kneading bread with their paws. Experts on cat behavior think there are good reasons for this behavior. Cats aren't trying to look like furry bakers. Kittens knead their mothers to get milk. Adult cats knead to mark objects with their scent.

## Make It Harder

Students who can summarize information in individual paragraphs can focus on summarizing the entire text that was used for Side A activities.

- For any paragraphs that have not yet been summarized, have partners use the steps on Side A to summarize the key idea and important information in a sentence.
- Then have partners combine the summary sentences for all paragraphs to summarize the entire text. Remind them to include only the key ideas and most important information in their own words. Tell them to delete or combine any repeated information.
- Have pairs share their text summaries with the class.

SIDE A

# Synthesize

As we read, we **synthesize,** or combine what we read with what we know to create a new understanding of the text, topic, or theme.

**COMPREHENSION**
GRADE 3

**Connect to *myView Literacy:***
**Synthesize Information:** Unit 2, p. T180

# ROUTINE

## STEP 1 INTRODUCE

When we synthesize, we use what we already know about the story or the topic plus information from our reading to reach new understandings.

## STEP 2 MODEL

- Choose and preview a familiar literary text. After previewing, I think about what I may already know about the text. Discuss what you already know about the text, including characters, setting, events, and the topic or theme.
- Read aloud the first section. As I read, I think about what I'm learning. I note details in the words and images. I combine the details to uncover new ideas or to think more deeply about the text. Discuss how new information leads to new understanding.
- Point out that readers keep synthesizing to the end of the text. When we finish reading, we combine the new information and think about the understandings we have now. What new ideas or lessons have we learned? How has our thinking changed?

## STEP 3 GUIDE PRACTICE

Read the rest of the text aloud. Use the points at the right to guide students to synthesize information and reach new understandings about the text, including about the setting, characters, and theme.

## STEP 4 ON THEIR OWN

Have students read a new, similar text. Have students explain how they combined the information in the words and images to think differently about the ideas in the text. Guide students as needed.

To synthesize, I . . .

- note what I already know about the characters, setting, topic, or theme.
- keep track of and include new information in the text and images as I read.
- note any new understandings I have.
- note how my thinking has changed from what I knew before I started reading the text.

SIDE B

# Synthesize

## CORRECTIVE FEEDBACK

**IF** students cannot synthesize information as they read,

**THEN** model how to synthesize information, using Steps 2 and 3. Next, work through the Make It Easier activity.

## Make It Easier

Students who struggle with synthesizing might need more support identifying new information in the details and images.

- Pick a familiar story with images that closely support the text. As we read, we can combine details in the text with details in the illustrations to learn more about a story.
- Read aloud a section of text. Discuss details in the text and how details in the illustrations support or clarify what is happening. For example, a version of "The Three Little Pigs" might include illustrations that show the different building materials each pig uses. By combining this information with text details, readers may come to the understanding that certain materials make sturdier, safer houses.
- Read through the text and note the images. Discuss examples of new information and ask students to share how the information changes their thinking about the characters, settings, or lessons in the story.

## Make It Harder

Students may enjoy synthesizing information about the same character in two different stories.

- Have partners read two different texts with the same main character, or different chapters in the same book.
- Before and as they read, have partners note details in the text and images that seem interesting or reveal something new about the character.
- When partners finish reading their texts or chapters, have them share their findings. Then have them synthesize three new understandings about the character that they came to based on their readings.

**SIDE A**

# Text Structure: Chronological/Sequence

**COMPREHENSION**
GRADE 3

**Connect to *myView Literacy:***
**Analyze Text Structure:** Unit 3, p. T240

**Text structure** is the organization of ideas an author uses in writing a text. A **chronological** text structure groups facts, ideas, or events into a **sequence,** or order, based on when they occurred in time.

## ROUTINE

### STEP 1 INTRODUCE

Text structure is how ideas or events are organized in a text. Chronological/sequence structure guides readers to see how events happen in time order. The events are organized from first to last.

### STEP 2 MODEL

- Display a familiar text organized in chronological order. Before I read the text, I preview and ask myself, *Do the text features or images show a time order? Are the paragraphs organized by event order?* Discuss what your preview reveals about the structure. After I preview, I start to read.
- Display the signal words. I'll look for these words as I read. Read aloud the first section, pointing out signal words. Signal words help me follow the chronological organization.
- Use questions such as those at the right to walk through the ideas or events in a section of the text. Then model using time order signal words to summarize the section.

Sequence Order

1. What happens first?
2. What happens next?
3. What happens last?

Signal Words

| | |
|---|---|
| first | after |
| next | then |
| before | finally |

### STEP 3 GUIDE PRACTICE

Read the rest of the text. Guide students to use the structure and signal words to discuss the order of events or ideas.

### STEP 4 ON THEIR OWN

Give students another brief chronological text. Have them preview and then read, noting how the sequential organization helps them follow the events or ideas.

COMPREHENSION
GRADE 3

SIDE B

# Text Structure: Chronological/Sequence

## CORRECTIVE FEEDBACK

| | |
|---|---|
| **IF** students cannot identify clues to chronological text structure, | **THEN** model the process, using Steps 2 and 3. Next, work through the Make It Easier activity. |

## Make It Easier

Students who struggle with chronological/sequence structure in a text might need more support identifying time order in a simple, clearly structured text.

- Display and preview the text at the right. The title tells me that this text is about the life of a butterfly. I know a life usually follows time order. For example, *First, I was born. Then I was a child. Finally, I grew to be an adult.*
- Read aloud the paragraph. The text says there are four parts of a butterfly's life. Let's underline signal words. These words tell the order.
- Reread each sentence and point to the signal word or phrase. Ask: What happens [first/next/after a while/finally]? as you read. List each event in a numbered list.
- Review the numbered list. Use the list to restate the events.
- Apply the process to other brief texts with sequence structure.

### A Butterfly's Life

The life of a butterfly has four main parts. First, a female adult butterfly lays an egg. Next, the egg hatches, and a caterpillar crawls out. After a while, the caterpillar forms into a pupa, or chrysalis. Finally, in a few weeks, an adult butterfly comes out of the pupa.

## Make It Harder

Students may enjoy mapping the sequence of events in a more challenging text.

- Have partners pick a text organized chronologically, such as a biography.
- Have partners take turns reading the text aloud and filling out a sequence chart to map events in the text. Note that many texts do not use sequence signal words throughout, requiring readers to pay closer attention to the order of events.
- Have partners use their completed sequence chart as well as signal words to summarize the events in order.

**SIDE A**

# Text Structure: Description

**COMPREHENSION**
**GRADE 3**

**Connect to *myView Literacy:***
**Informational Text:** Unit 5, p. T85

A **description** text structure explains, defines, or illustrates a topic or a concept.

## ROUTINE

### STEP 1 INTRODUCE

A description helps readers understand what something is like. Description text structure guides readers by grouping the traits, features, or characteristics of a topic, thing, or idea.

### STEP 2 MODEL

- Display a familiar descriptive text. First, I preview. I ask, *Do photos or diagrams show what something is like? Do the headings or paragraphs work together to describe something?* Discuss what is being described.
- Read aloud the first section of the text. As I read, I look for words that signal a description. Display the signal words and phrases. Often these signal words introduce an example. Discuss how the signal words provide clues to help you answer questions such as the ones in the box at the bottom right.
- Point out how the structure helps reveal the text's main points. Walk through the structure to identify what is being described in the first section of the text. What is being described? How are the traits or features organized here?

Signal Words and Phrases
for example
such as
for instance
in addition
also
too

Description
- What is it like?
- What does it look like?
- What is it made of?
- How does it work?

### STEP 3 GUIDE PRACTICE

Read the rest of the text. Guide students to identify other descriptions and use the structure and signal words to answer the questions at the right. How do the descriptions support the main points?

### STEP 4 ON THEIR OWN

Give students another brief descriptive text. Have them preview and then read the text. Have them explain how the structure and any examples help clarify the author's main points.

# Text Structure: Description

COMPREHENSION
GRADE 3

## CORRECTIVE FEEDBACK

**IF** students cannot identify clues to the description text structure,

**THEN** model how to identify different parts of a description, using Steps 2 and 3. Next, work through the Make It Easier activity.

## Make It Easier

Students might need more support identifying descriptions.

- Display and preview the text. I see the text has a title and two paragraphs. The title is "Inside a Prairie Dog Home." What do you think it will describe? (what prairie dog homes are like inside)
- Read aloud the first paragraph. What does this paragraph tell us? (A prairie dog home is underground. It has a tunnel with chambers.)
- Read the second paragraph. How does this paragraph connect to the first one? Point to "for example" and "this particular room." Explain that these words signal additional information. How does this information add to the description? (It tells more about one type of room.)
- Guide students to use the information in the text to explain what a prairie dog home is like.

### Inside a Prairie Dog Home

Prairie dogs live underground. Their homes include a tunnel connecting different rooms called chambers.

Each chamber has a purpose. For example, one is used as a nursery. This particular room is where prairie dogs care for their young.

## Make It Harder

Students may benefit from adding text features and visuals to emphasize the descriptive structure of the text about prairie dog homes.

- Have partners reread the text. Then, have them add a heading to the second paragraph that would help readers follow the structure.
- Next, have partners create a diagram to illustrate what the text describes.
- Have partners present their completed texts and visuals, explaining how the new features help readers better understand the text's main points.

**COMPREHENSION**
GRADE 3

SIDE A

# Text Structure: Steps in a Process

**Connect to *myView Literacy:***
**Explain Use of Text Structure:**
Unit 5, p. T174

**Steps in a process** text structure guides readers through a sequence of steps to understand how something is done or made.

## ROUTINE

### STEP 1 INTRODUCE

Texts such as a recipe or a science experiment explain a process—how something is done or made. They usually have numbered steps. The numbers show the sequence, or order, of the parts of the process.

### STEP 2 MODEL

- Display a familiar process text with numbered steps. I start with a preview. I ask, *Do pictures or diagrams show a process? Are there headings or numbered steps that are clues to steps in a process?* Identify the process.
- Many procedural texts start with an introduction and list of materials. Read aloud the introduction and materials list.
- The steps are listed in order, and they are usually numbered. Point out that authors may also use time-order signal words to show sequence. Discuss why it's important to follow steps of a process in order.
- Read the rest of the text. Pause to discuss any diagrams or images. Explain how they help you understand the process.

Steps in a Process
- What process is explained?
- What materials are needed?
- Are there numbered steps or signal words?
- What do I do first? Next? Last?

Signal Words
first
next
before
after
finally

### STEP 3 GUIDE PRACTICE

Reread the whole text. Guide students to use the steps or signal words to discuss the order and how the process works.

### STEP 4 ON THEIR OWN

Give students another brief procedural text, such as a how-to text. Have them preview and read it, noting how steps and text features help them identify the structure and understand the process.

**SIDE B**

# Text Structure: Steps in a Process

**COMPREHENSION**
**GRADE 3**

**CORRECTIVE FEEDBACK**

**IF** students cannot identify clues to the process text structure,

**THEN** model how to identify and follow steps in order, using Steps 2 and 3. Next, work through the Make It Easier activity.

## Make It Easier

Students might need more support following steps in order.

- Find and display a simple how-to text, such as how to grow a plant from an avocado pit. Read aloud the entire text. Discuss how the numbers help you identify structure. Ask questions such as, *Why wouldn't it make sense to do step 3 first? Why do we follow the steps in order?*
- Now provide students with the materials for the process. Use the text to prompt students to complete each step. Ask: What is the first step? What do you do next? Now what do you do? What step comes last?
- Then have students present their completed project. Have them use the steps to explain how they completed it.

How to Grow an Avocado Plant

**Materials:** avocado pit, jar of water, toothpicks

1. Dry the pit and stick toothpicks into it.
2. Put the pit in the jar, wide side down (under water).
3. Put the jar in the sun.
4. Once the sprout grows to 3", replant it in soil.

## Make It Harder

Students may benefit from practice following the steps in an authentic text.

- Provide students with a how-to text that shows a process they can complete with classroom materials. Have partners read the text, gather materials, and follow instructions to complete the process.
- Have partners use their completed project and the text to explain what they did. Ask students to explain how images or signal words in the text helped them follow the process. Encourage them to discuss whether or not the steps were clear and easy to follow, and why.

**SIDE A**

# Text Structure: Cause and Effect

**COMPREHENSION**
GRADE 3

A **cause-and-effect** text structure is used to show how one event, a cause, causes another event, an effect.

**Connect to *myView Literacy:***
**Analyze Text Structure:** Unit 2, p. T298

## ROUTINE

### STEP 1 INTRODUCE

A cause-and-effect text structure helps readers see how one event causes another event. The cause is what happens first. The effect is the event that happens because of the first event. A cause-and-effect text structure guides readers to see the relationship between events.

| Cause | → | Effect |
|---|---|---|

### STEP 2 MODEL

- Display an informational text with cause-and-effect structure. Before I read, I preview. I ask, *Do the headings or images suggest that one event causes another event? Does one paragraph present a cause and another the effect(s)?* Preview the text features and arrangement of paragraphs.
- Read aloud the first section. As I read, I look for words that signal causes and effects. Display the signal words. Point out signal words in the text and explain that they help show how events are connected.
- Discuss how noting the connections between causes and effects helps you understand the key ideas in the text.

**Signal Words**
so
since
because
as a result

### STEP 3 GUIDE PRACTICE

Reread the text, guiding students to analyze other causes and their effects to better understand the relationships between events.

### STEP 4 ON THEIR OWN

Give students another brief cause-and-effect text. Have them identify clues to the structure before and as they read and explain how the structure helps them understand how events are connected.

# Text Structure: Cause and Effect



**CORRECTIVE FEEDBACK**

**IF** students cannot identify clues to cause-and-effect text structure,

**THEN** model how to identify causes and effects, using Steps 2 and 3. Next, work through the Make It Easier activity.

## Make It Easier

Students who struggle with cause-and-effect text structure might need more support identifying how one event (a cause) makes another event (an effect) happen.

- Display the text at the right. I read the title. This is a news story about a forest fire. The fire caused a forest to burn down. The fire is the cause. *What did it cause?* (The forest burned.) That is the effect.
- What caused the fire? Read aloud the first two sentences. Underline *caused.* I see the word *caused.* That is a clue.
- Use the following frame: ______ caused ______ to happen. *What event happened first?* (lightning) *What event happened because of this event?* (a forest fire) The lightning caused the fire. Lightning is the cause. The fire is the effect.
- Read the rest of the text, identifying the signal words and filling in the frame to show more causes and effects.

**Fire Burns Down Forest**

A bolt of lightning struck a tree in the West End Woods yesterday. The lightning caused a forest fire to start. Because the winds were so strong, the fire grew. As a result, West End Woods burned down.

## Make It Harder

Students who are able to identify cause-and-effect structure may benefit from completing a flow chart to show the chain of events in a real-life news story. Provide partners with a text about an appropriate event in your school or town.

- Provide a flow chart graphic organizer, such as the following.

- Have partners read the text and note the cause-and-effect chain in the chart. Then, have them use the completed chart to summarize the story.

# Teacher Resources

# Articulation Support Guide

## Sound Articulation

Articulation is the formation of clear and distinct sounds. Teaching articulation along with phonological awareness benefits children and helps them become accurate and fluent readers. In fact, research shows a direct correlation between phonological awareness and reading success.

- Children must learn to isolate and pronounce the sounds, or phonemes, in spoken words.
- Children must map the sounds (phonemes) of English to letters or groups of letters (graphemes) that spell the sounds.
- To read successfully, children must access the sounds that the graphemes represent, read (decode) the words, and relate to the meaning of the words (comprehend).

With appropriate instruction that includes articulation support, children can become both accurate and fluent readers. Current research supports combining seeing, hearing, and saying to help children master sound-spellings and sound articulation.

## Routine Sound Articulation

This routine can be used for teaching sound articulation or for reteaching children who need additional support.

1. **Introduce** Display the sound-spelling and tell children the name of the sound spelling.

*Examples*
- Display the letter *f*. Say: The name of this letter is f.
- Display the digraph *ch*. Say: This is the consonant digraph ch.

2. **Model** Say the sound and tell children how to articulate the sound.

*Examples*
- When you say /f/, your top teeth touch your bottom lip.
- When you say /ch/, the tip of your tongue touches the roof of your mouth. Then air is released.

3. **Practice** Display the sound-spelling. Ask children to name the sound-spelling. Then ask children to produce the sound.

# Distinguishing Similar Sounds

Some sounds can be difficult for children to distinguish. The sounds are produced almost identically, but there is a slight difference such as a variation in mouth formation, slightly different tongue position, or use of the vocal cords. For example, one sound might be voiced, meaning that the vocal cords vibrate when that sound is being produced, and the other might be unvoiced, meaning that there is no vocal cord vibration.

Here are examples of sounds that children can sometimes confuse.

## Consonant Cognates

| Unvoiced | Voiced |
|---|---|
| /f/ | /v/ |
| /p/ | /b/ |
| /t/ | /d/ |
| /k/ | /g/ |
| /s/ | /z/ |
| /th/ | /TH/ |

## Vowels

| Sounds | Difference |
|---|---|
| /e/ and /i/ | Both are voiced, but tongue position is different. |
| /e/ and /ɑ/ | Both are voiced, but mouth position is different. |
| /e/ and /ā/ | Both are voiced, but mouth position is different. |

## Other Commonly Confused Sounds

| Sounds | Difference |
|---|---|
| /ch/ and /sh/ | Both are unvoiced, but air is released differently. |
| /m/ and /n/ | Both are voiced, but mouth position is different. |

## Routine Distinguishing Similar Sounds

Use this routine to help children distinguish sounds that are often confused.

**1 Introduce** Tell children that some sounds can be tricky because they sound a lot alike.

*Examples*

- Telling the difference between the sounds /f/ and /v/ can be tricky because they sound a lot alike.
- Telling the difference between /e/ and /i/ can be tricky because they sound a lot alike.

**2 Model** Explain how producing the sounds is similar and different.

*Examples*

- When I say both /f/ and /v/, my top teeth touch my bottom lip. The difference is how the air comes out of my mouth. When I say /f/, the air just flows through my lips. Put your hand on your throat. When I say /v/, the air flows through my lips, but I can also feel my throat move.
- When I say both /e/ and /i/, my jaw is open. When I say /e/, my tongue is slightly rounded up. When I say /i/, my tongue is slightly lowered.

**3 Practice** Have children practice producing the two sounds.

*Examples*

- Put a hand on your throat. Say /f/ and /v/. Notice how your throat moves when you say /v/ but not when you say /f/.
- Say /e/ and /i/. Notice how your tongue is in a different position when you say each sound.

# Articulation Instruction for the Sounds of English

## Consonant Sounds

| Sound | Pronunciation | Sample Words | Voiced? |
|---|---|---|---|
| /b/ | When you say /b/, you put your lips together. Then your lips open and a tiny puff of air comes out of your mouth. | ball, bat, bike | Voiced |
| /k/ | When you say /k/, the back of your tongue is humped in the back of your mouth. | cat, kite, kangaroo | Unvoiced |
| /d/ | When you say /d/, the tip of your tongue touches above your top teeth. | duck, dress, donut | Voiced |
| /f/ | When you say /f/, your top teeth touch your bottom lip. | fox, fish, fan, phone | Unvoiced |
| /g/ | When you say /g/, your mouth is open and your tongue is humped at the back of your mouth. | goose, gold, guitar | Voiced |
| /h/ | When you say /h/, your mouth is open and air is pushed out of your mouth. | hammer, hat, hairbrush | Unvoiced |
| /j/ | When you say /j/, the tip of your tongue touches the roof of your mouth. Then air is released. | juice, jellyfish, gym | Voiced |
| /l/ | When you say /l/, the tip of your tongue touches above your top teeth and stays there. | lamp, lion, lemon | Voiced |
| /m/ | When you say /m/, your lips come together. | moon, muffin, mouse | Voiced |
| /n/ | When you say /n/, your tongue is at the top of your mouth behind your teeth and a little air comes out of your nose. | nest, notebook, napkin | Voiced |

*continued*

***continued*** **Consonant Sounds**

| Sound | Pronunciation | Sample Words | Voiced? |
|---|---|---|---|
| /p/ | When you say /p/, your lips start out together. They then open and a puff of air comes out of your mouth. | pillow, pinecone, pretzel | Unvoiced |
| /kw/ | When you say /kw/, the back of your tongue is humped in the back of your mouth, and then your lips come together in a small circle. | queen, quilt, question mark | Voiced |
| /r/ | When you say /r/, the tip of your tongue goes up toward the roof of your mouth. | rake, rainbow, rocket | Voiced |
| /s/* | When you say /s/, your tongue is near the top of your front teeth. Your tongue stays there as air is pushed out of your mouth. | sing, sandwich, sun | Unvoiced |
| /t/ | When you say /t/, the tip of your tongue touches above your top teeth, and then a tiny puff of air comes out of your mouth. | tomato, toad, tent | Unvoiced |
| /v/ | When you say /v/, your top teeth touch your bottom lip. | volcano, van, vegetable | Voiced |
| /w/ | When you say /w/, your lips form a small circle. | web, wagon, walrus | Voiced |
| /ks/ | When you say /ks/, the back of your tongue is humped in the back of your mouth and then moves to touch your bottom teeth as your jaw closes. | fox, box, socks | Unvoiced |
| /y/ | When you say /y/, your tongue starts near the roof of your mouth and then moves down. | yellow, yo-yo, yogurt | Voiced |
| /z/* | When you say /z/, your tongue is near the top of your front teeth. Your tongue stays there as air is pushed out of your mouth and sound comes out. | zipper, zebra, zucchini | Voiced |

*In plurals with the ending *-s*, unvoiced /s/ follows unvoiced sounds such as /p/ and /t/ and voiced /z/ follows voiced sounds such as /g/.

## Short Vowel Sounds

| Sound | Pronunciation | Sample Words | Voiced? |
|---|---|---|---|
| /ɑ/ | When you say /ɑ/, your jaw and tongue are down. | alligator, ant, apple | Voiced |
| /e/ | When you say /e/, your jaw is open and tongue is slightly rounded up. | elephant, egg, envelope | Voiced |
| /i/ | When you say /i/, your mouth is open and your tongue is slightly lowered. | iguana, igloo, insect | Voiced |
| /o/ | When you say /o/, your mouth is open and your jaw drops. | octopus, otter, olive | Voiced |
| /u/ | When you say /u/, your mouth is open, and your tongue is down. | umbrella, up, umpire | Voiced |

## Long Vowel Sounds

| Sound | Pronunciation | Sample Words | Voiced? |
|---|---|---|---|
| /ā/ | When you say /ā/, start with your tongue in the middle of your mouth. Your tongue moves up as your jaw closes slightly. | acorn, cake, skates | Voiced |
| /ē/ | When you say /ē/, your tongue is high in your mouth and your jaw is almost closed. | eagle, tree, seal | Voiced |
| /ī/ | When you say /ī/, your tongue is low in your mouth. It moves upward as your jaw closes. | island, five, lime | Voiced |
| /ō/ | When you say /ō/, your lips form a circle that gets smaller as your jaw closes slightly. | oatmeal, rope, rose | Voiced |
| /ū/ | When you say /ū/, you begin with your tongue near the roof of your mouth. Then the front of your tongue lowers as you close your lips into a small circle. | unicorn, music, cube | Voiced |
| /ü/ | When you say /ü/, your lips form a small circle and the back of your tongue is high. | balloon, flute, raccoon | Voiced |

## Consonant Digraph Sounds

| Sound | Pronunciation | Sample Words | Voiced? |
|---|---|---|---|
| /ch/ | When you say /ch/, the tip of your tongue touches the roof of your mouth. Then air is released. | chick, chocolate, peach | Unvoiced |
| /sh/ | When you say /sh/, your lips stick out and air is pushed out. | shark, shell, sheep | Unvoiced |
| /th/ | When you say /th/, you put the tip of your tongue between your top and bottom teeth. Then air comes out of your mouth. | thumb, thorn, tooth | Unvoiced |
| /TH/ | When you say /TH/, you put the tip of your tongue behind your top front teeth. Your tongue and teeth may touch lightly and your vocal cords vibrate to make sound. | the, then, smooth | Voiced |
| /hw/ | When you say /hw/, your lips form a small circle as air is pushed out. | whale, whiskers, whistle | Unvoiced |
| /ng/ | When you say /ng/, the back of your tongue lifts up and touches the back of your mouth. | string, ring, king | Voiced |
| /ngk/ | When you say /ngk/, the back of your tongue lifts up and touches the back of your mouth. Your vocal cords vibrate as sound is produced, and then sound is cut off as a puff of air is released. | skunk, wink, pink | Voiced |
| /zh/ | When you say /zh/, your lips stick out. The sides of your tongue might touch your top teeth. | treasure, television, measure | Voiced |

## *r*-Controlled Vowel Sounds

| Sound | Pronunciation | Sample Words | Voiced? |
|---|---|---|---|
| /ɑr/ | When you say /ɑr/, your tongue is low in your mouth and then moves up as your jaw closes. | star, marker, car | Voiced |
| /ėr/ | When you say /ėr/, you lift the back of your tongue so that the sides of your tongue touch the back teeth. | bird, word, turtle | Voiced |
| /ôr/ | When you say /ôr/, you begin with your lips in a small circle. Then your lips open and your tongue rises. | fork, corn, horse | Voiced |

## Diphthongs and Other Vowel Sounds

| Sound | Pronunciation | Sample Words | Voiced? |
|---|---|---|---|
| /oi/ | When you say /oi/, you begin with your lips in a small circle. Then your lips open and your tongue rises and comes forward. | toy, boy, coin | Voiced |
| /ou/ | When you say /ou/, you begin with your jaw open and your tongue low near your teeth. Then you close your jaw and form your lips into a circle. | owl, cloud, mouse | Voiced |
| /u̇/ | When you say /u̇/, your lips form a relaxed circle and the back of your tongue lifts up. | bull, bush, pudding | Voiced |
| /ȯ/ | When you say /ȯ/, you push your tongue back and low, and your lips are rounded. | hawk, straw, lawn mower | Voiced |

**A note about initial consonant blends:** When encoding words with two-consonant blends in beginning position, including blends that are commonly confused with other spellings, children should distinguish the placement and action of the lips, teeth, and tongue during articulation.

# Glossary

**abbreviation:** A shortened form of a longer word or phrase, using some letters from the original word or words

**accuracy:** To read a text correctly, without omitting, adding, or changing any of the words

**analogy:** A type of figurative language that compares something unknown to something familiar; a comparison of pairs of unlike items having something in common

**antonym:** A word with a meaning that is opposite to the meaning of another word

**ask and answer questions:** A process in which readers ask and answer questions about the text before, during, and after reading to deepen understanding and gain information

**base word:** The simplest form of a word; it can stand alone, or endings or affixes may be added

**build background knowledge:** To connect one's own background to a text for better understanding of the text, and then to add more knowledge from the text during reading

**cause and effect:** A text structure that shows how one event, a *cause,* causes another event, an *effect*

**chronological:** A text structure that groups facts, ideas, or events into a sequence, or order, based on when they occurred

**closed syllable:** A syllable that ends with a consonant and usually has a short vowel sound

**compound word:** A word made of two or more smaller words

**context clue:** A type of hint, such as a synonym, an antonym, an example, or a brief definition, found within a text that helps readers figure out the meaning of an unfamiliar word

**contraction:** A shortened form of two words in which some letters are removed and replaced with an apostrophe

**decodable high-frequency words:** High-frequency words which have sound-spelling patterns that have been previously learned

**description:** A text structure that explains, defines, or illustrates a topic or a concept

**detail:** A small, often interesting piece of information that tells more about a main idea in a text

**diphthong:** A single vowel sound, represented by two letters, that resembles a glide from one sound to another

**drama/play:** A type of writing that tells a story and is acted out for others

**figurative language:** Language used for descriptive effect that gives words a meaning beyond their dictionary definition

**final stable syllable:** An unaccented syllable, such as a consonant + *-le, -tion,* or *-sion,* that always appears at the end of a word

**high-frequency words:** The words that appear most often in our written language

**homograph:** A word that is spelled the same as another word but is different in meaning and often pronunciation

**homophone:** A word that has the same pronunciation as another word but is different in spelling and meaning

**inference:** A smart guess that readers make by combining what they know with details they read

**inflected ending:** A letter or group of letters added to a base word that changes the word's tense, voice, or number

**informational text:** A type of writing with a main idea and details that provides facts and information about a topic

**irregular plural noun:** A noun that does not follow the usual pattern of adding *-s* or *-es* to form the plural; it may involve spelling changes or no change at all

**literary text:** A type of writing that tells a story or entertains

**main idea:** The most important idea, or big idea, about a topic in a text or section of text

**metaphor:** A type of figurative language that makes a comparison between unlike things without using *like* or *as*

**monitor comprehension:** To use different strategies to confirm understanding during reading

**multisyllabic word:** A word that has more than one syllable

**narrative text:** Any type of writing, including fiction or nonfiction, that relates a series of events

**non-decodable high-frequency words:** High-frequency words which do not follow a regular sound-spelling pattern *or* the sound-spelling patterns have not been previously learned

**open syllable:** A syllable that ends with a long vowel sound

**oral vocabulary:** Words used in speaking or recognized when listening

**phoneme addition:** The ability to say a new word by adding a phoneme (sound) to a word

**phoneme blending:** The ability to recognize and identify a sequence of spoken sounds and combine them to form a word

**phoneme chaining:** An exercise in which one sound is manipulated to make each new word in a list of words

**phoneme deletion:** The ability to say the word that remains when a specific phoneme is removed

**phoneme isolation:** The ability to identify and say a particular phoneme in a word apart from the rest of the word

**phoneme manipulation:** The ability to modify, change, or move sounds within words or syllables

**phoneme matching:** The ability to recognize and identify phonemes that are the same in initial, final, or medial positions in words or syllables

**phoneme reversal:** The ability to say the sounds of a word backwards to create a new word

**phoneme segmentation:** The ability to break a word into its individual sounds, or phonemes

**phonemic awareness:** The ability to hear, think about, and work with the individual sounds (phonemes) in spoken words

**prediction:** A smart guess that readers make about what a text might be about or what might happen next based on details in the text

**prefix:** A word part added to the beginning of a word that changes the meaning of the word

**prosody:** Oral reading with appropriate phrasing, intonation, and emphasis

**rate:** Oral reading at the speed of natural speech, demonstrating automatic word recognition and smooth pacing

***r*-controlled vowel:** A single vowel followed by the letter *r* that has neither a long vowel sound nor a short vowel sound, but an *r*-controlled vowel sound

**resource:** A print or an online source, such as a glossary, dictionary, or thesaurus, that gives the meanings of words

**rhyme:** Two or more words with the same middle and ending sounds

**rhyming word:** See *rhyme*.

**rhythm:** The pattern of stressed and unstressed syllables

**schwa:** The vowel sound in an unstressed syllable that is neither long nor short

**self-monitor:** To listen as you read to notice and correct word-reading errors and to confirm understanding

**sequence:** See *chronological*.

**simile:** A type of figurative language that compares two unlike things using *like* or *as*

**steps in a process:** A text structure that guides readers through a sequence of steps to understand how something is done or made

**suffix:** A word part added to the end of a word that changes the word's meaning, part of speech, or both

**summarize:** To restate in one's own words the most important ideas or events of a text in a shorter version of the original

**surrounding text:** The words and sentences near an unfamiliar word

**syllable:** A word part that has one vowel sound

**synonym:** A word with a meaning that is similar to the meaning of another word

**synthesize:** To combine ideas in a text with what the reader already knows to create a new understanding of a text, topic, or theme

**text structure:** The organization of ideas an author uses when writing a text

**thesaurus:** A resource that lists words and their synonyms

**VC*e* syllable:** When a syllable has a vowel-consonant-silent e pattern, the vowel usually stands for its long sound (e.g., tape, Pete, fine, rope, cute)

**vowel digraph:** Two letters that spell one vowel sound

**vowel pattern:** See *vowel digraph*.

**vowel team:** See *vowel digraph*.

**word part:** A base word, root, prefix, or suffix with a specific meaning that contributes to the meaning of a word

# Research

Anderson, Nancy A. and Elizabeth L. Kaye. "Finding Versus Fixing: Self-Monitoring for Readers Who Struggle." *The Reading Teacher* 70 (2017): 543–550.

Baker, Scott, Nonie Lesaux, Madhavi Jayanthi, Joseph Dimino, C. Patrick Proctor, Joan Morris, Rebecca Newman-Gonchar, et al. "Teaching Academic Content and Literacy to English Learners in Elementary and Middle School" (NCEE 2014-4012). Washington, D.C.: National Center for Education Evaluation and Regional Assistance (NCEE), Institute of Education Sciences, U.S. Department of Education.

Castles, Anne, Kathleen Rastle, and Kate Nation. "Ending the Reading Wars: Reading Acquisition from Novice to Expert." *Psychological Science in the Public Interest* 19, no. 1 (June 2018): 5–51.

Dehaene, Stanislas. "How the Brain Learns to Read." Filmed November 14, 2012, at Doha, Qatar. Video, 33:29.

Dehaene, Stanislas. "The Reading Brain: What Every Educator Needs to Know." Accessed August 20, 2020. http://education.ohio.gov/getattachment/Topics/Learning-in-Ohio/Literacy/Striving-Readers-Comprehensive-Literacy-Grant1/2020-Literacy-Academy/1-06-2-06-The-Reading-Brain-Lit-Academy-ACCESSIBLE-PDF-1.pdf.aspx?lang=en-US.

Duke, Neil K., David P. Pearson, and Alessandra E. Ward. "The Science of Reading Comprehension Instruction." *The Reading Teacher* 74, no. 6 (2021): 663–672.

Ehri, Linnea C., Simone R. Nunes, Steven A. Stahl, and Dale M. Willows. "Systematic Phonics Instruction Helps Students Learn to Read: Evidence from the National Reading Panel's Meta-Analysis." *Review of Educational Research* 71, no. 3 (September 2001): 393–447.

Ehri, Linnea C. "Orthographic Mapping in the Acquisition of Sight Word Reading, Spelling Memory, and Vocabulary Learning." *Scientific Studies of Reading* 18, no. 1 (2014): 5–21.

Elleman, Amy M., Endia J. Lindo, Paul Morphy, and Donald L. Compton. "The Impact of Vocabulary Instruction on Passage-Level Comprehension of School-Age Children: A Meta-Analysis." *Journal of Research on Educational Effectiveness* 2, no. 1 (2009): 1–44.

Eunice Kennedy Shriver National Institute of Child Health and Human Development, NIH, DHHS. "Report of the National Reading Panel: Teaching Children to Read: Reports of the Subgroups" (00-4754). Washington, D.C.: U.S. Government Printing Office, 2000.

Hanford, Emily. "At a Loss for Words: How a Flawed Idea Is Teaching Millions of Kids to Be Poor Readers." APM Reports (American Public Media), August 22, 2019.

Jeynes, William H. "A Meta-Analysis of the Relationship Between Phonics Instruction and Minority Elementary School Student Academic Achievement." *Education and Urban Society* 40, no. 2 (January 2008): 151–166.

Kilpatrick, David A. *Equipped for Reading Success.* Syracuse, New York: Casey & Kirsch Publishers, 2016.

Kilpatrick, David A. *Essentials of Assessing, Preventing, and Overcoming Reading Difficulties.* Hoboken, NJ: Wiley, 2015.

Kovelman, Ioulia, Elizabeth S. Norton, Joanna A. Christodoulou, Nadine Gaab, Daniel A. Lieberman, Christina Triantafyllou, Maryanne Wolf, Susan Whitfield-Gabrieli, and John D. E. Gabrieli. "Brain Basis of Phonological Awareness for Spoken Language in Children and Its Disruption in Dyslexia." *Cerebral Cortex* 22, no. 4 (April 2012): 754–764.

Lee, Jiyeon, and So Yoon Yoon. "The Effects of Repeated Reading on Reading Fluency for Students with Reading Disabilities: A Meta-Analysis." *Journal of Learning Disabilities* 50, no. 2 (March 2017): 213–224.

Marulis, Loren M., and Susan B. Neuman. "The Effects of Vocabulary Intervention on Young Children's Word Learning: A Meta-Analysis." *Review of Educational Research* 80, no. 3 (September 2010): 300–335.

Miles, Katharine P., Gregory B. Rubin, and Selenid Gonzalez-Frey. "Rethinking Sight Words: The Interaction Between Students' Phonics Knowledge and Words' Spelling Regularity." *The Reading Teacher* 71, no. 6 (2018): 715–726.

Moats, Louisa C. "Teaching Reading Is Rocket Science: What Expert Teachers of Reading Should Know and Be Able to Do." *American Educator* (Summer 2020).

Morgan, Paul L., and Georgios D. Sideridis. "Contrasting the Effectiveness of Fluency Interventions for Students with or at Risk for Learning Disabilities: A Multilevel Random Coefficient Modeling Meta-Analysis." *Learning Disabilities Research & Practice* 21, no. 4 (November 2006): 191–210.

Pearson, P. David, Annemarie S. Palincsar, Gina Biancarosa, and Amy I. Berman, eds. "Reaping the Rewards of the Reading for Understanding Initiative." Washington, D.C.: National Academy of Education, 2020.

Petscher, Yaacov, Sonia Q. Cabell, Hugh W. Catts, Donald L. Compton, Barbara R. Foorman, Sara A. Hart, Christopher J. Lonigan, Richard Wagner, et al. "How the Science of Reading Informs 21st-Century Education." *Reading Research Quarterly* (September 2020): S267–S282.

Piasta, Shayne B., and Richard K. Wagner. "Developing Early Literacy Skills: A Meta-Analysis of Alphabet Learning and Instruction." *Reading Research Quarterly* 45, no. 1 (January/February/March 2010): 8–38.

Seidenberg, Mark S. "The Science of Reading and Its Educational Implications." *Language Learning and Development* 9, no. 4 (2013): 331–360.

Seidenberg, Mark S. "What Has Research Taught Us About How Children Learn to Read?" Interview with Reading Rockets. January 25, 2019. Video, 3:18.

Shanahan, Timothy. "The National Reading Panel Report: Practical Advice for Teachers." Learning Point Associates / North Central Regional Educational Laboratory (NCREL), 2005.

Shanahan, Timothy. "The Science of Reading: Improving Reading Achievement." Accessed August 20, 2020. https://www.shanahanonliteracy.com/publications/the-science-of-reading.

Suggate, Sebastian P. "A Meta-Analysis of the Long-Term Effects of Phonemic Awareness, Phonics, Fluency, and Reading Comprehension Interventions." *Journal of Learning Disabilities* 49, no. 1 (January 2016): 77–96.

Swanborn, M. S. L., and K. de Glopper. "Incidental Word Learning While Reading: A Meta-Analysis." *Review of Educational Research* 69, no. 3 (September 1999): 261–285.

Therrien, William J. "Fluency and Comprehension Gains as a Result of Repeated Reading: A Meta-Analysis." *Remedial and Special Education* 25, no. 4 (July 2004): 252–261.

Toste, Jessica R., Kelly J. Williams, and Phillip Capin. "Reading Big Words: Instructional Practices to Promote Multisyllabic Word Reading Fluency." Hammill Institute on Disabilities. (2016).

Wolf, Maryanne. "The Deep-Reading Brain and the Good Life." Accessed August 20, 2020. https://medium.com/thrive-global/the-deep-reading-brain-and-the-good-life-3f9ec5e5a4c0.

# Teacher Notes

# Teacher Notes

# Teacher Notes

# Teacher Notes

# Teacher Notes

# Teacher Notes

# Teacher Notes